Consider the lilies,
how they grow:
they neither toil
nor spin;
but I tell you,
not even Solomon
in all his glory
clothed himself
like one of these.

Luke 12:27

Flowers for you!

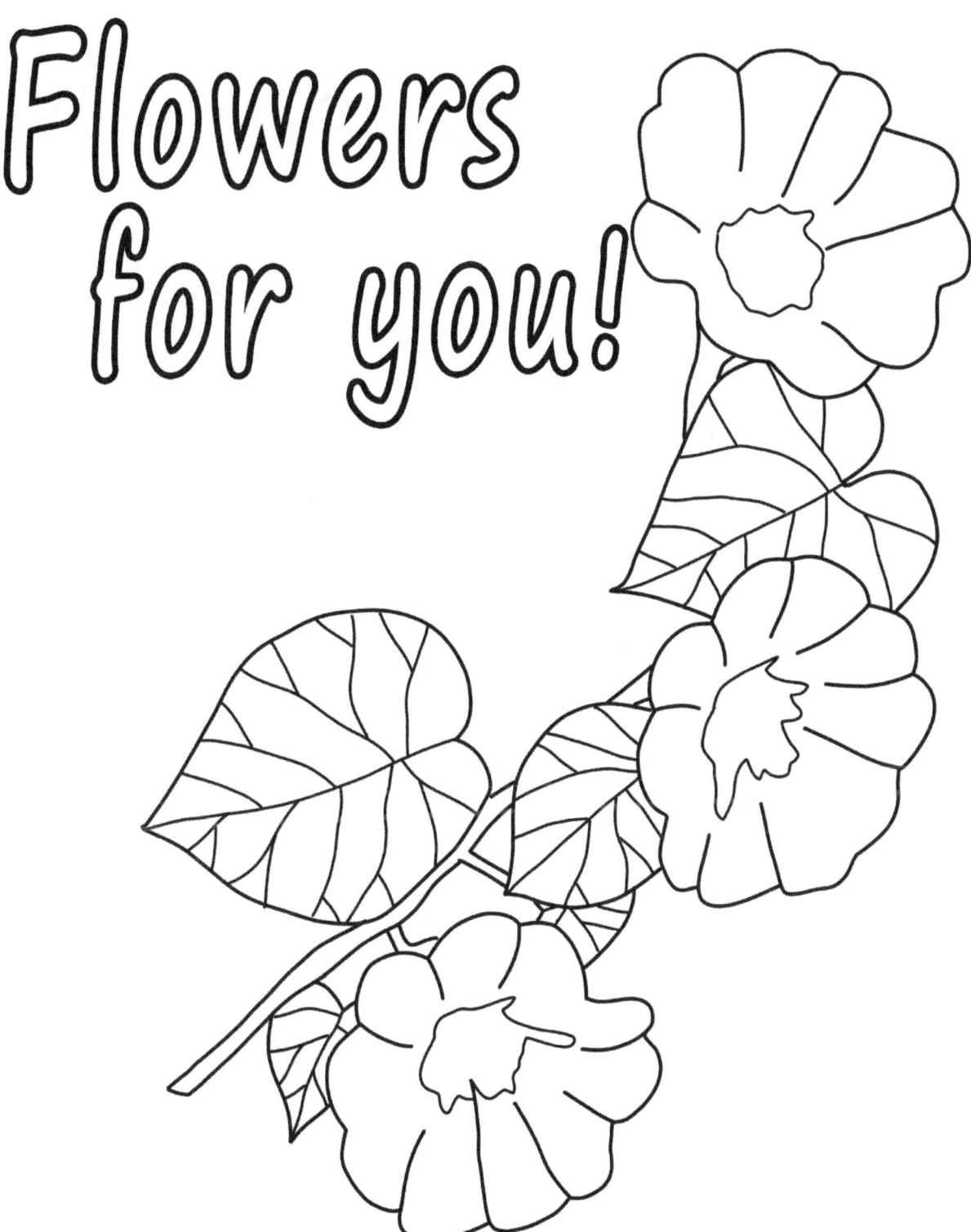

Lupita Romo
Adult Coloring Book
For beginners, seniors and individuals with low vision

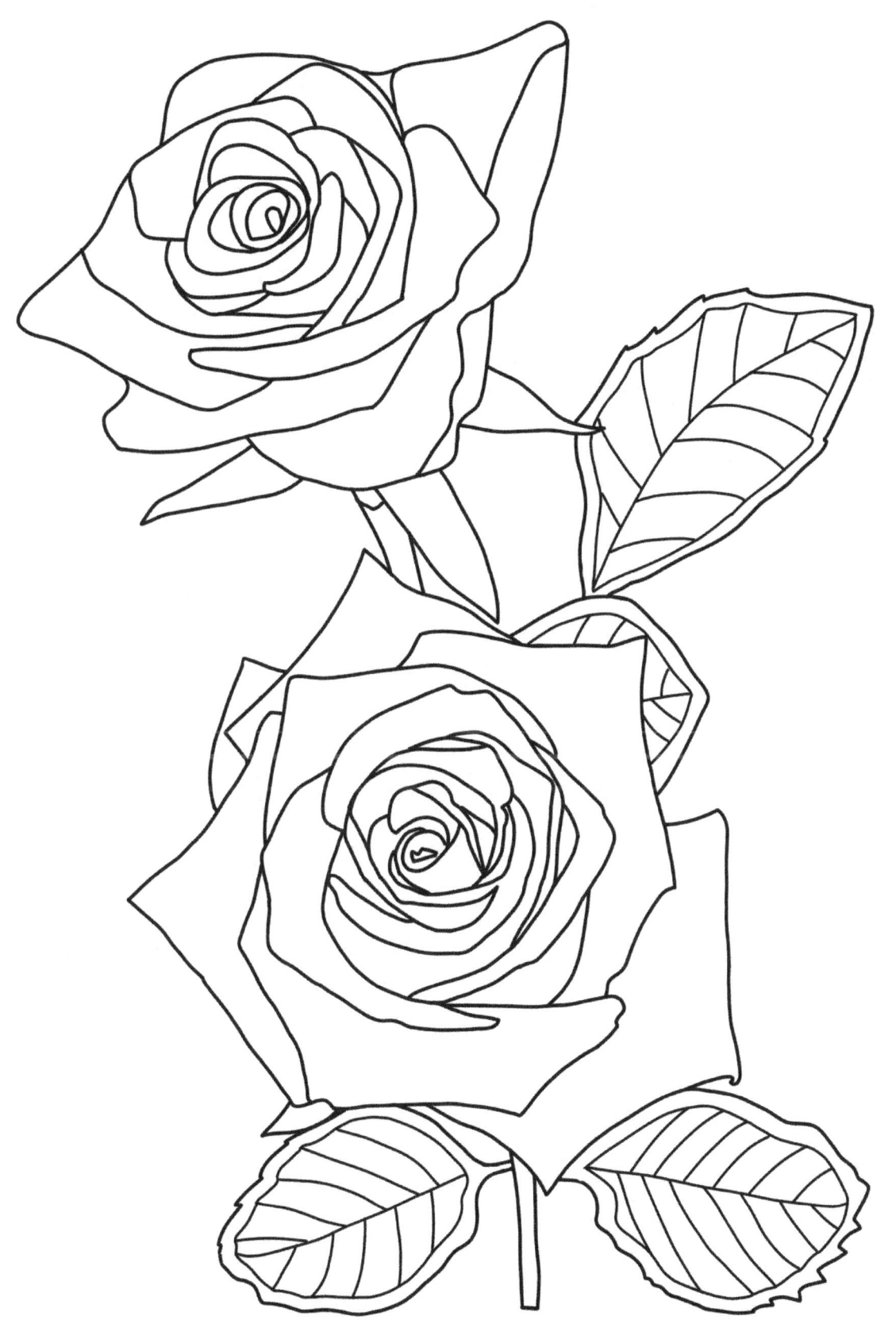

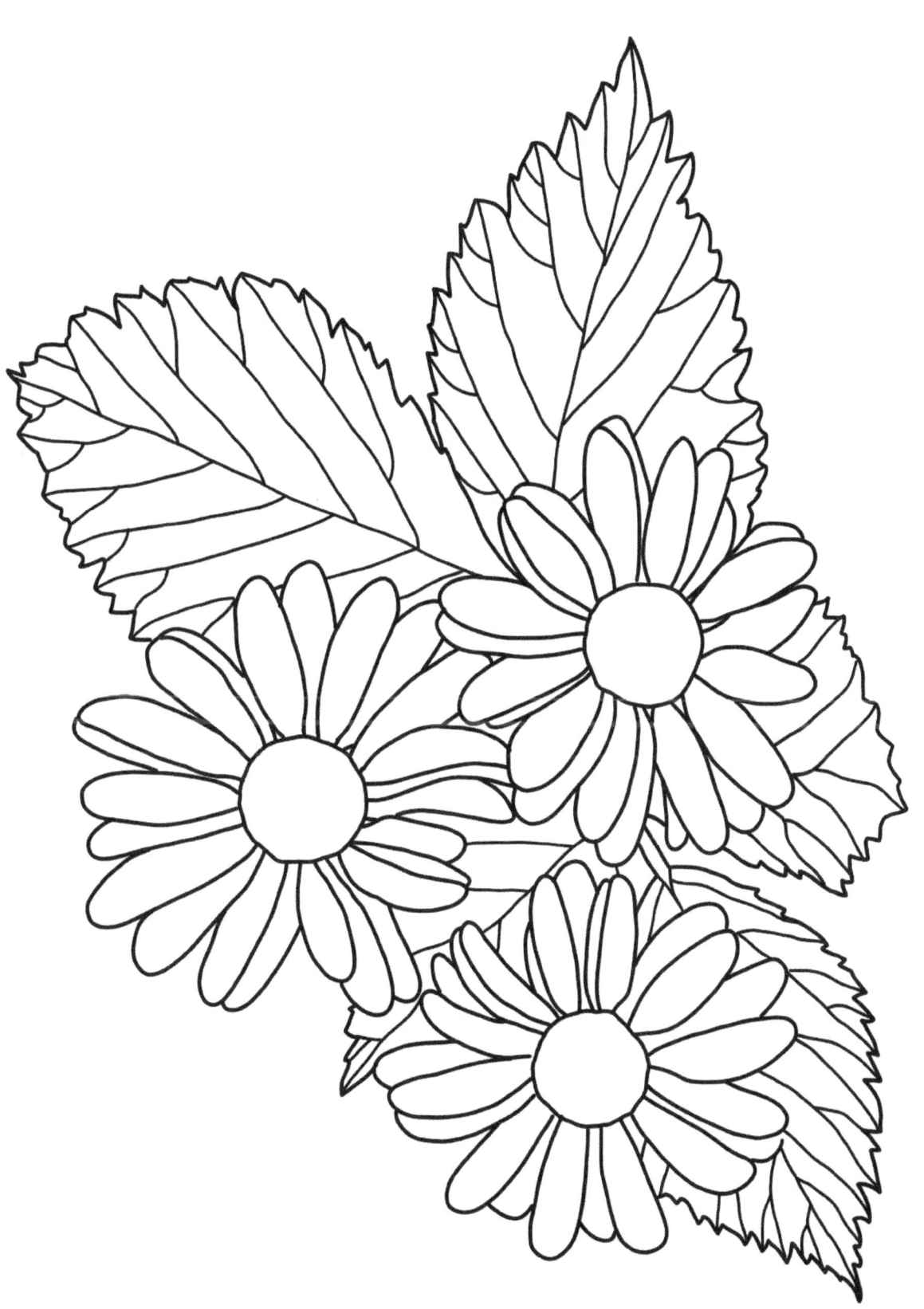

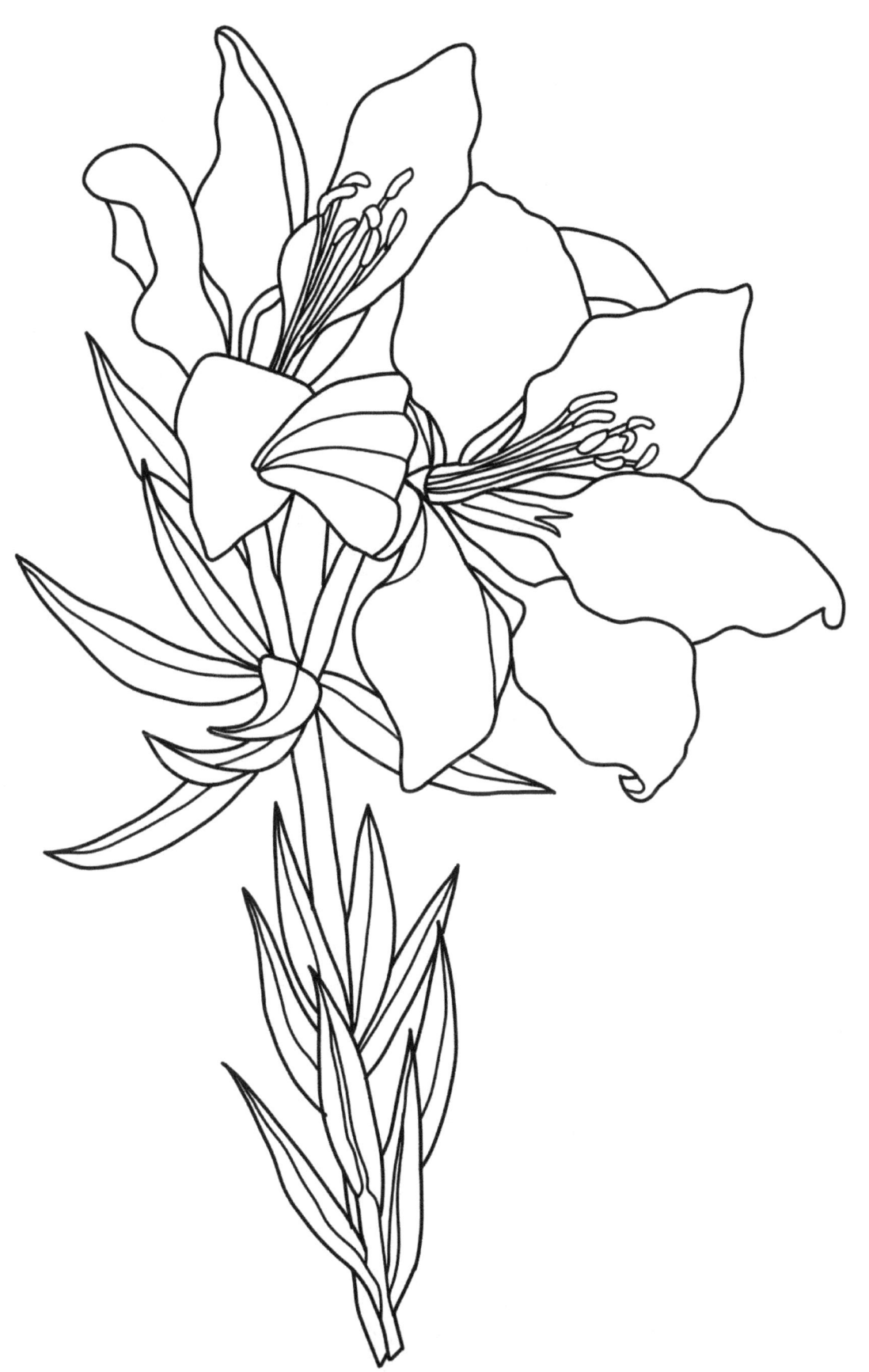

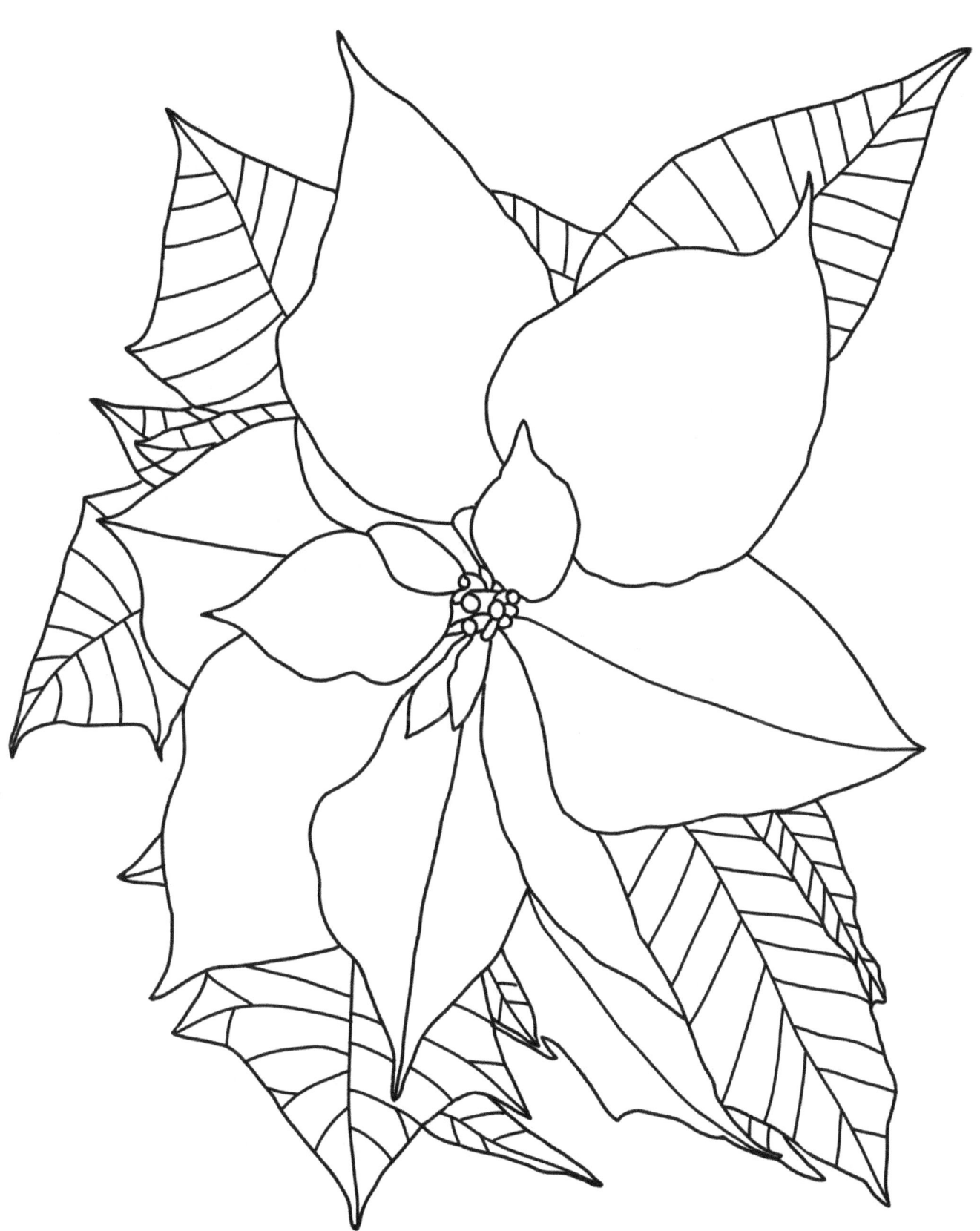

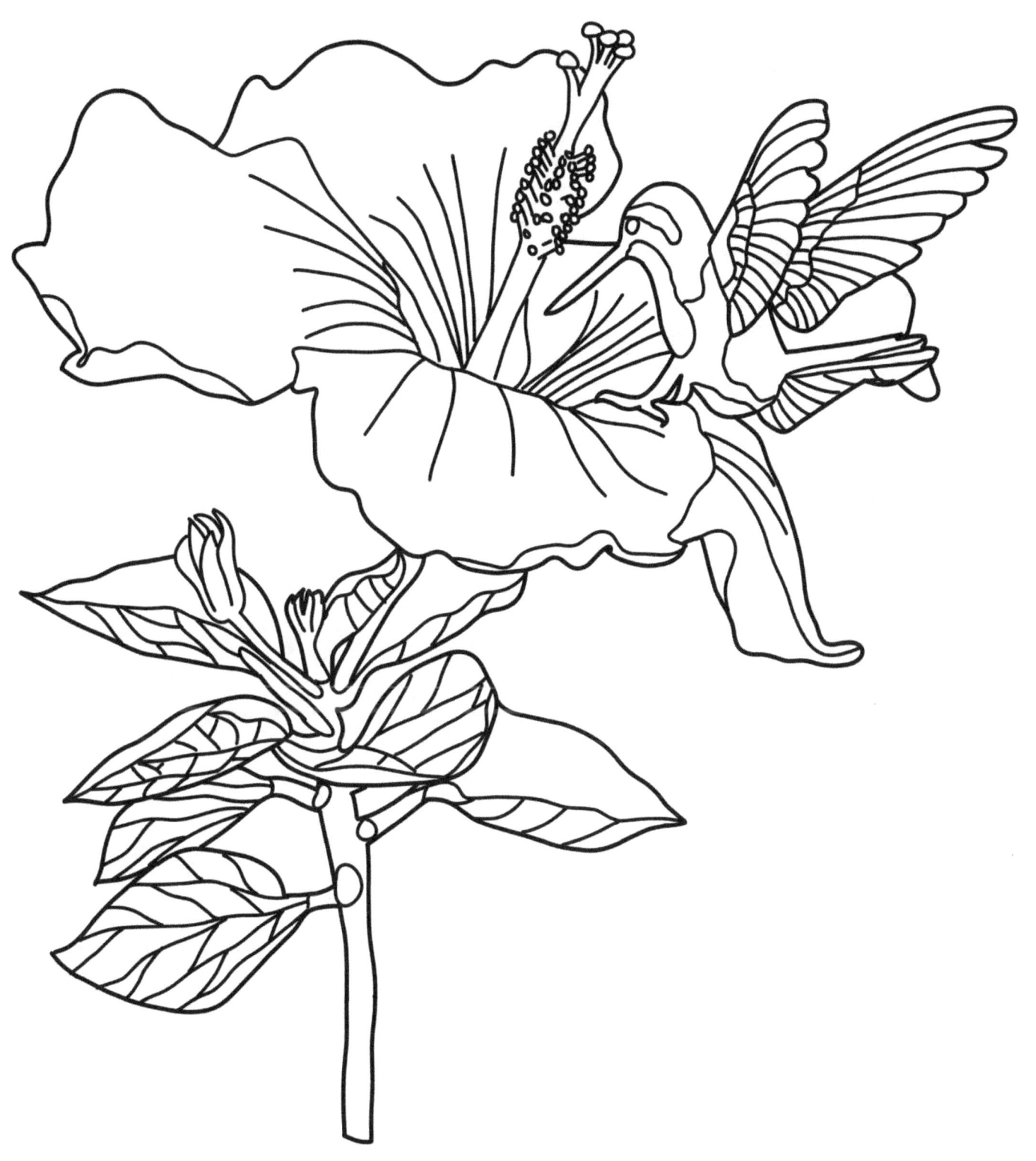

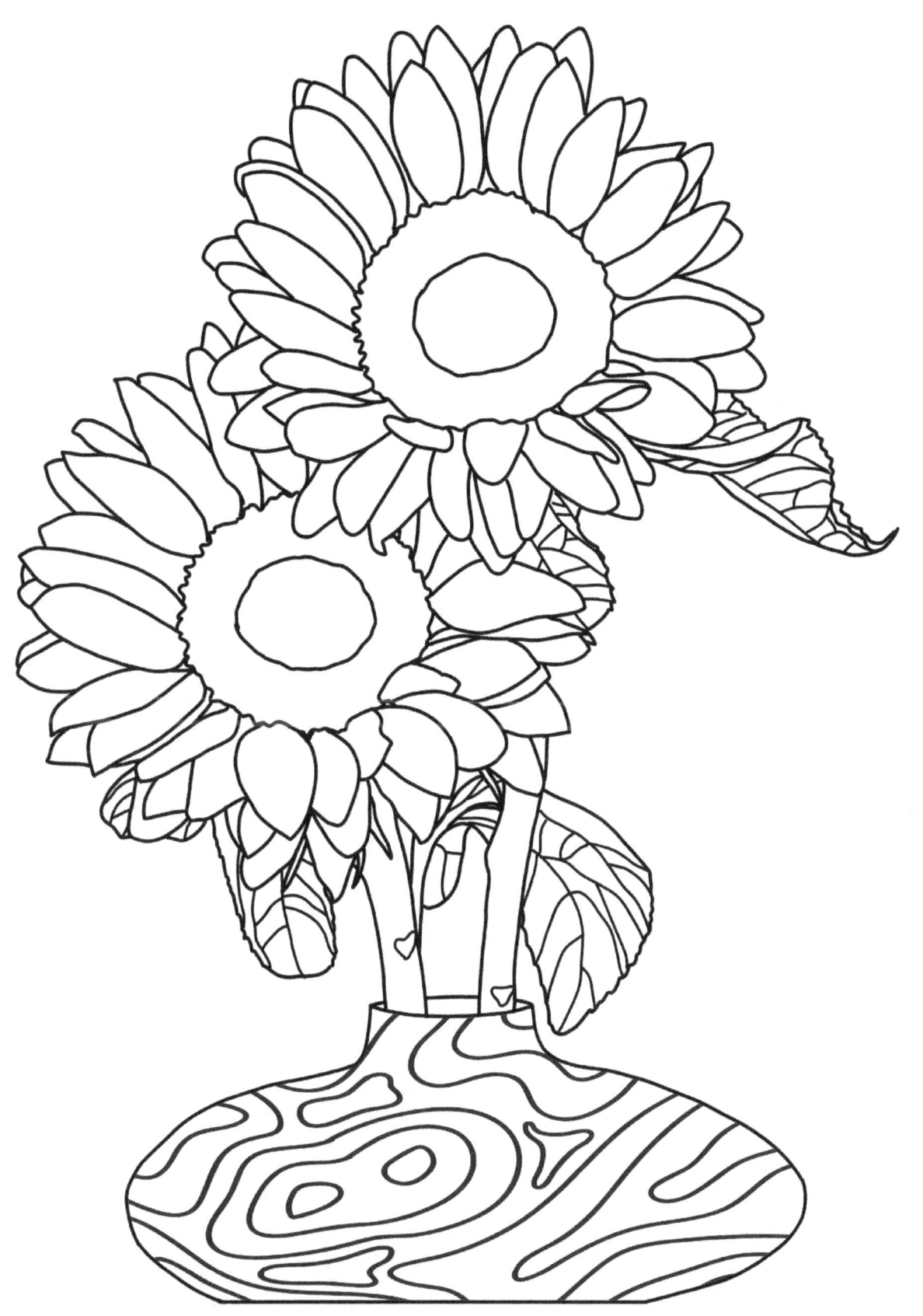

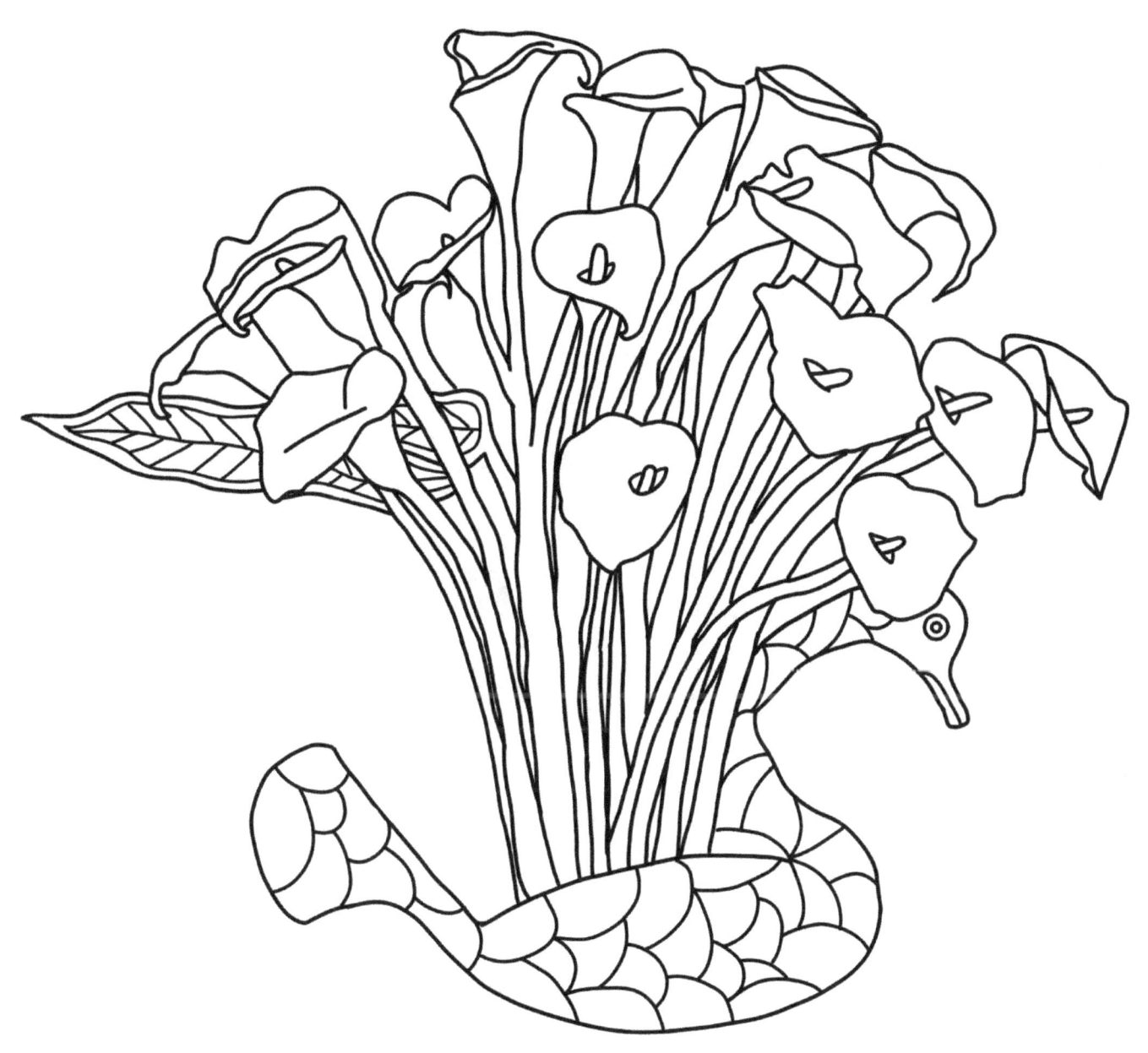

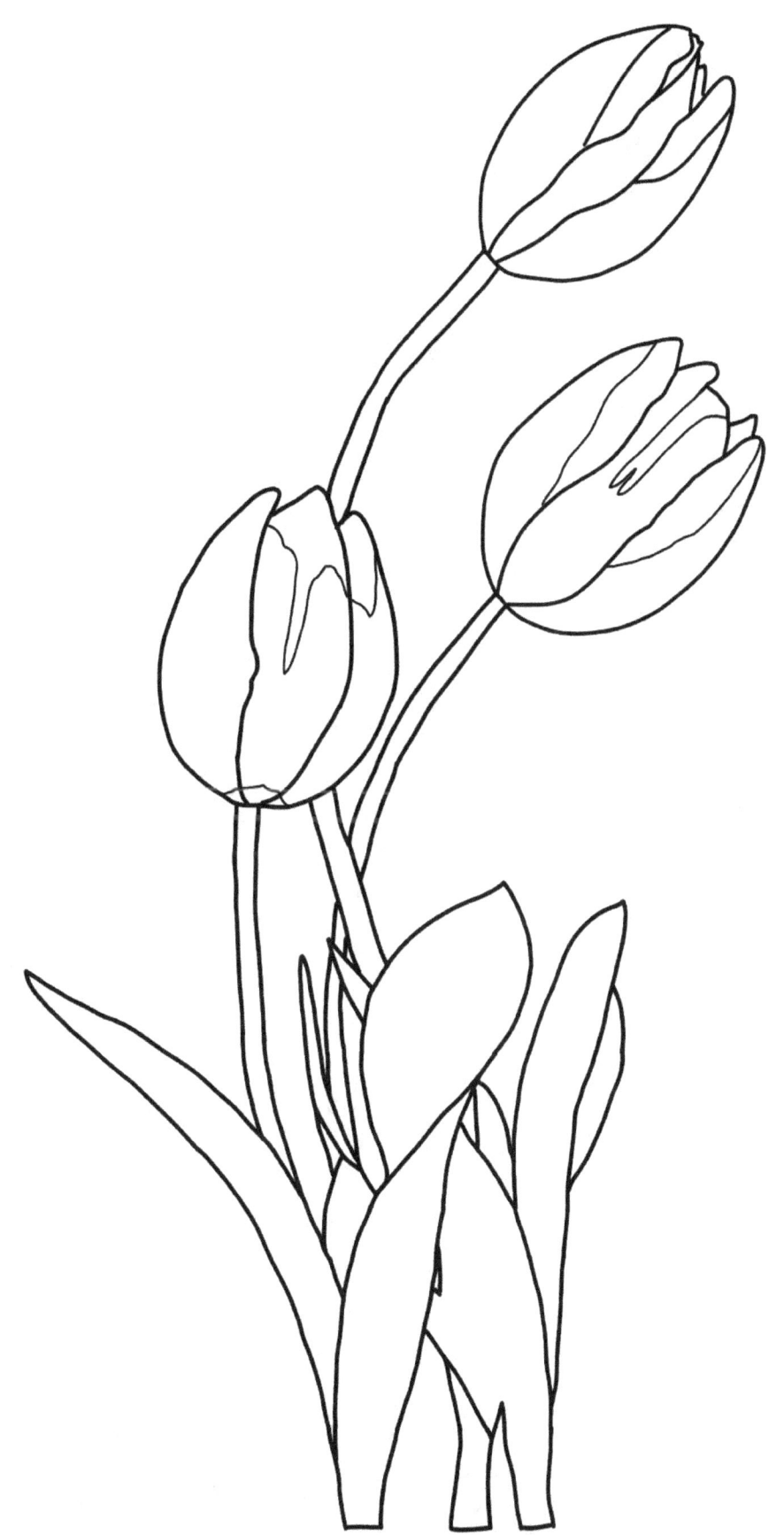

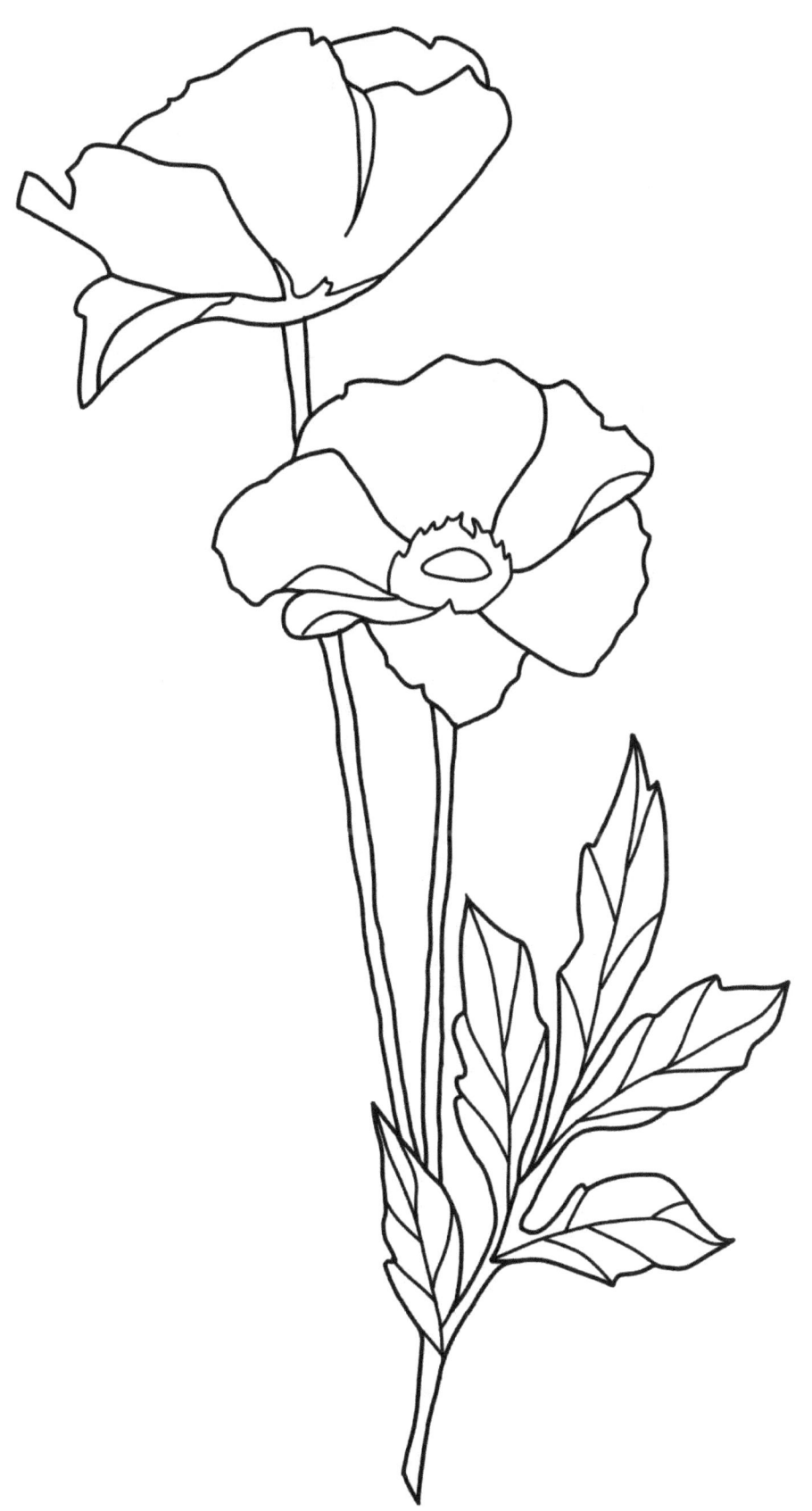

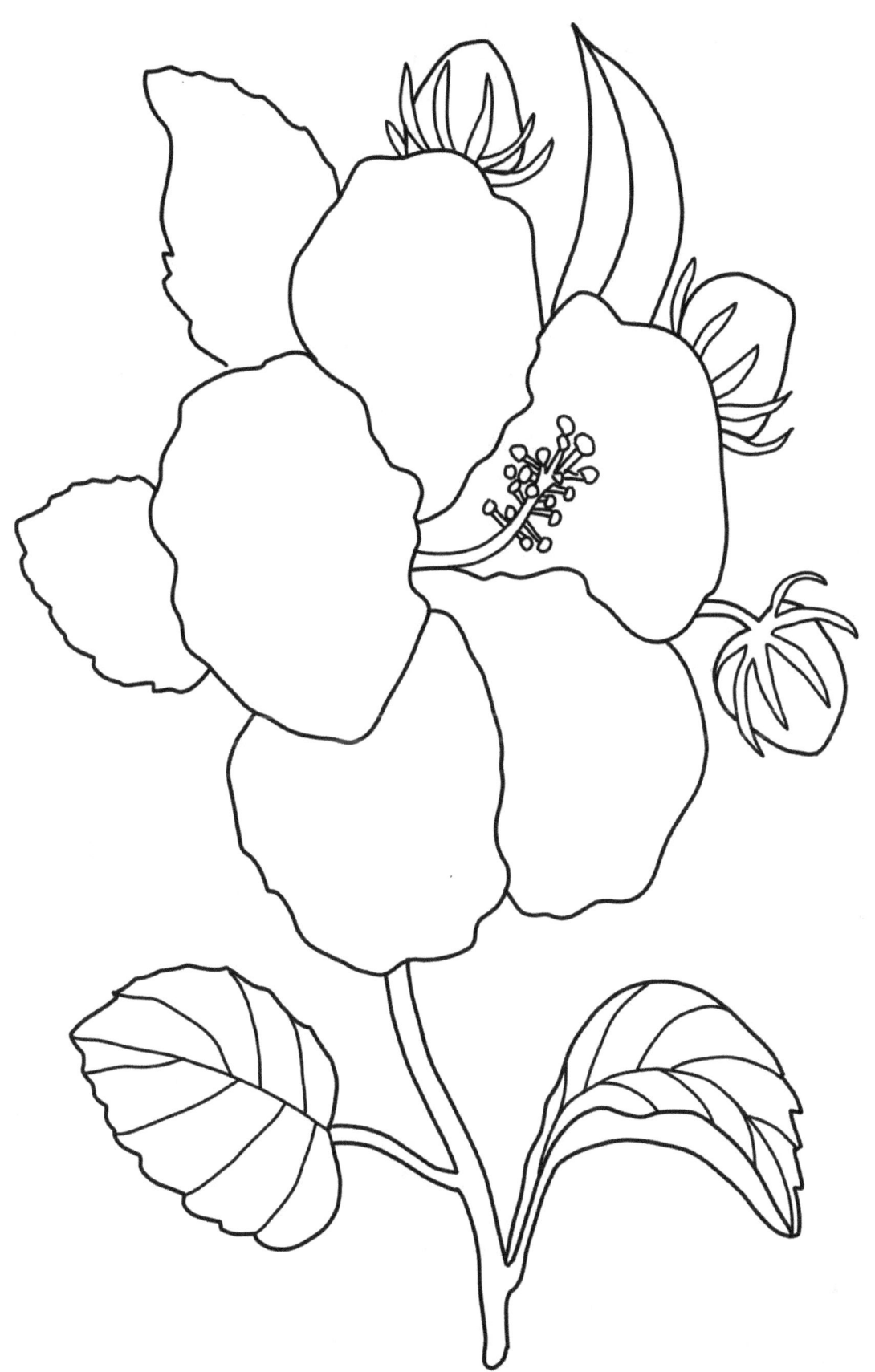

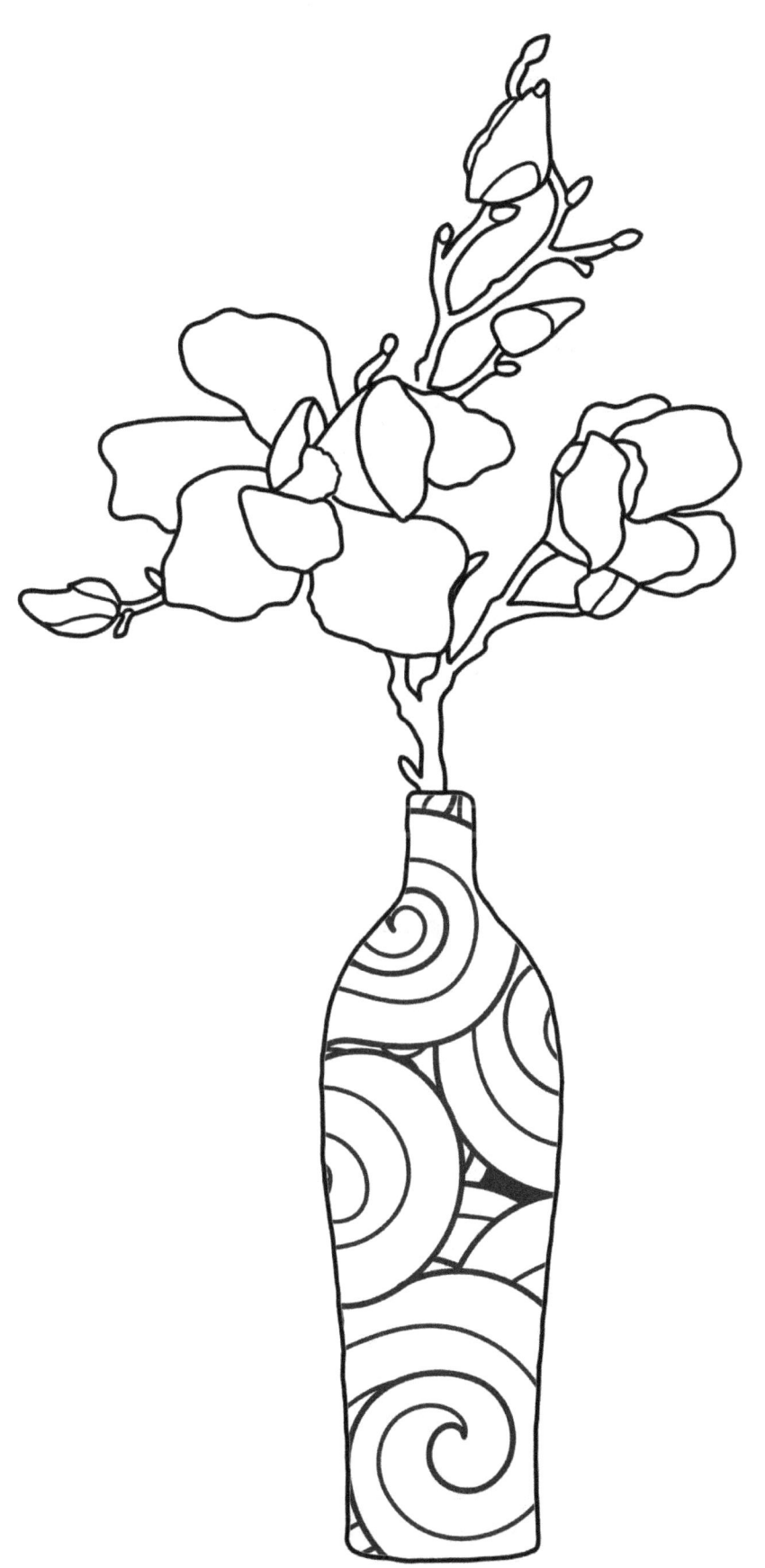

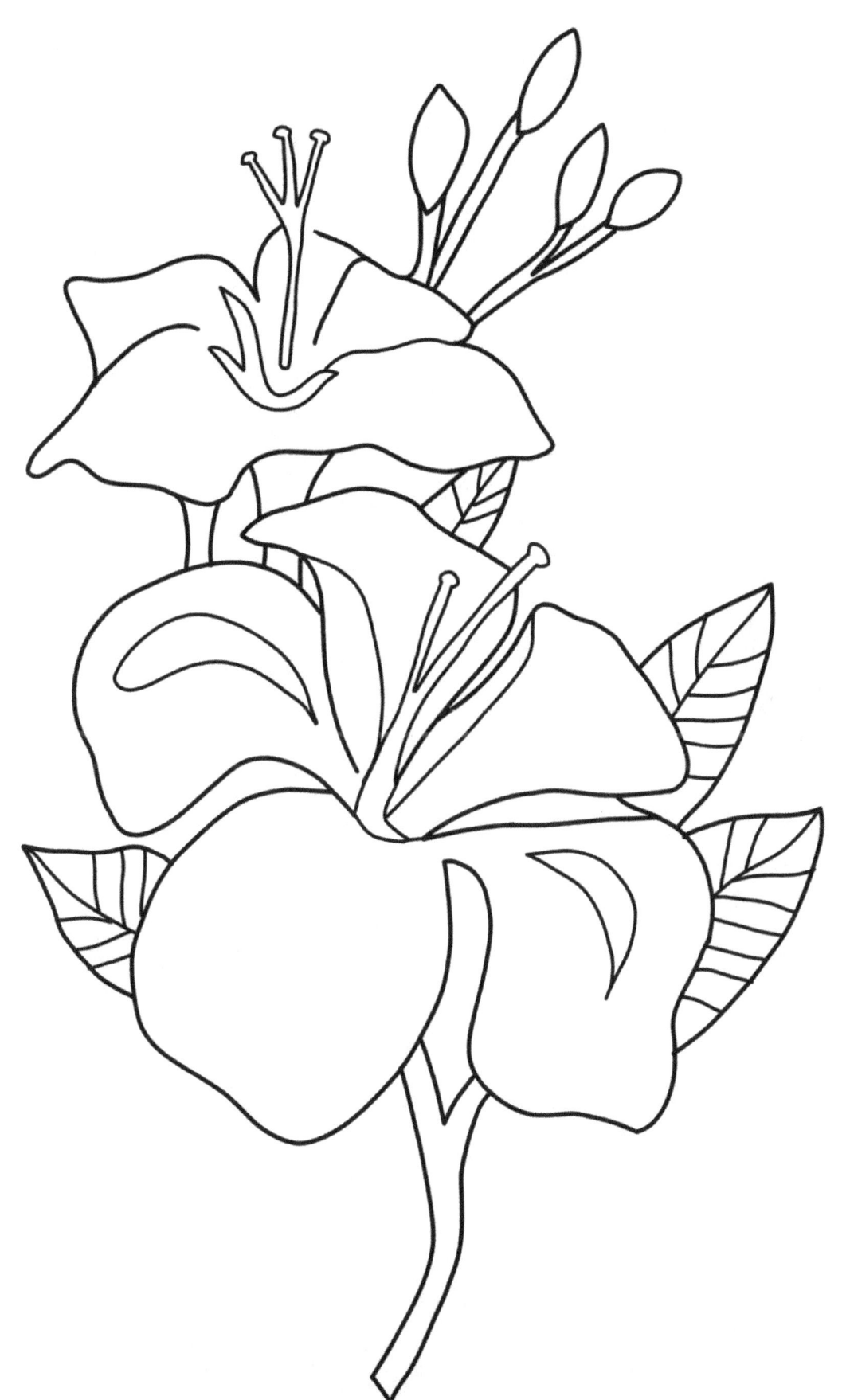

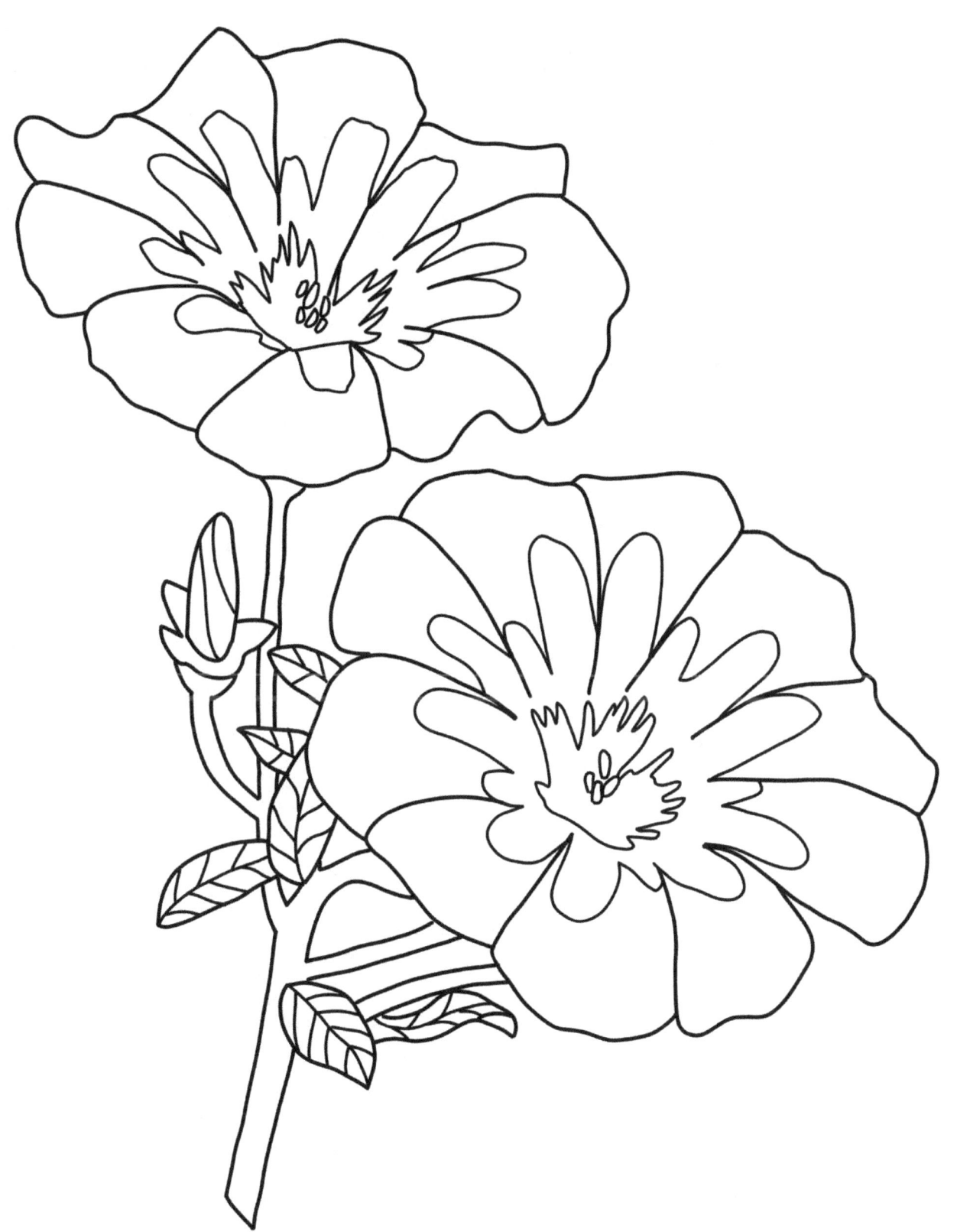

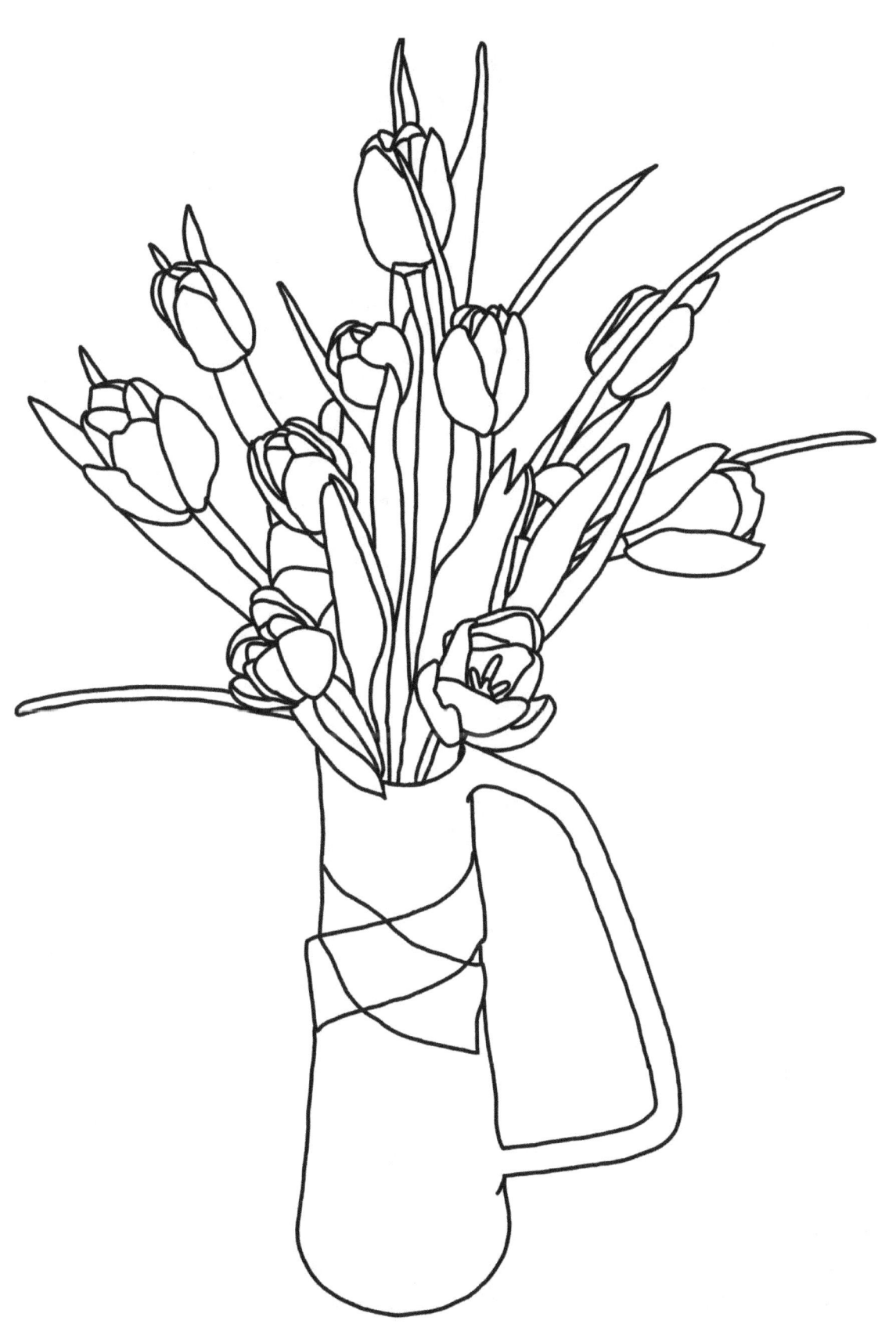

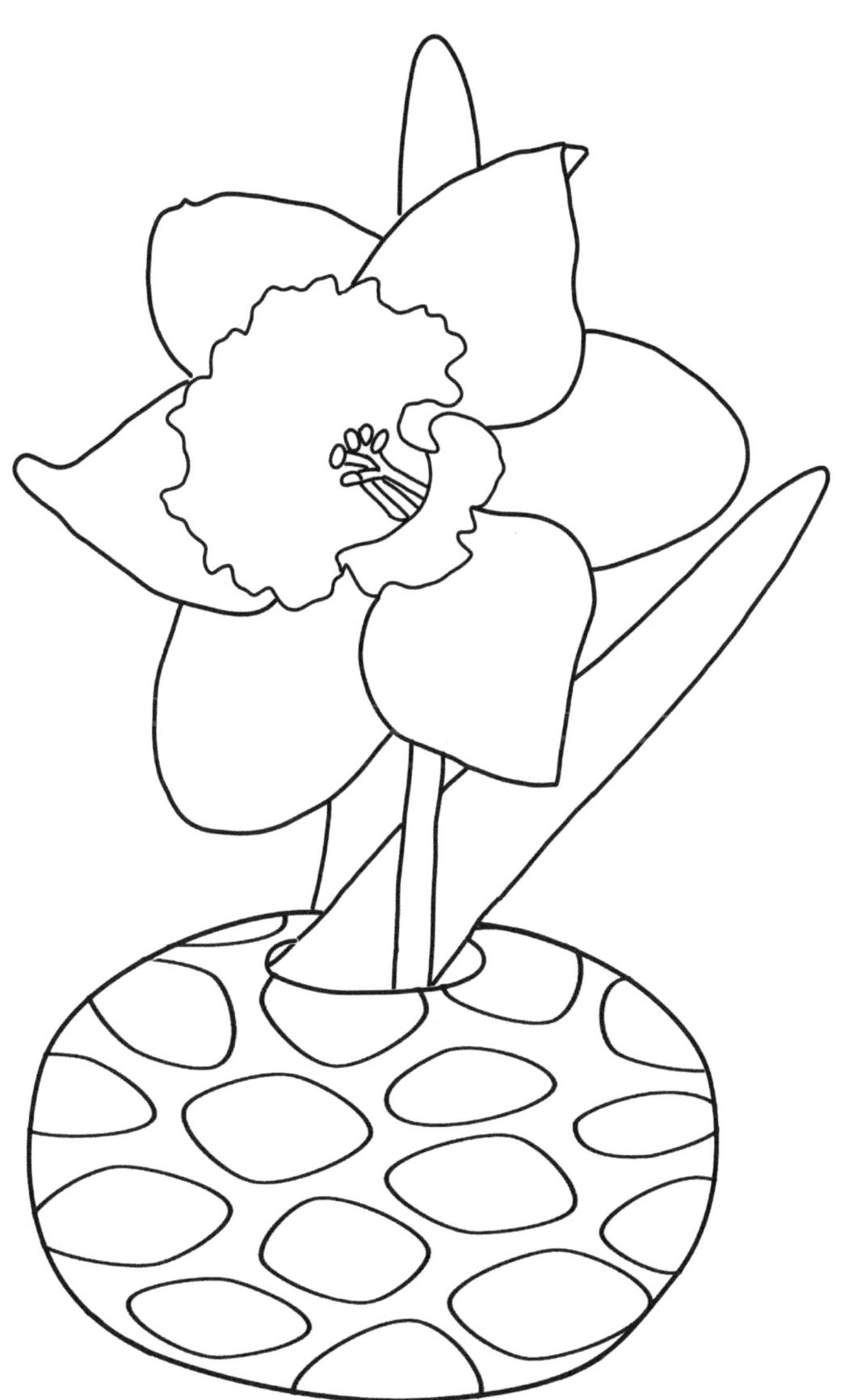

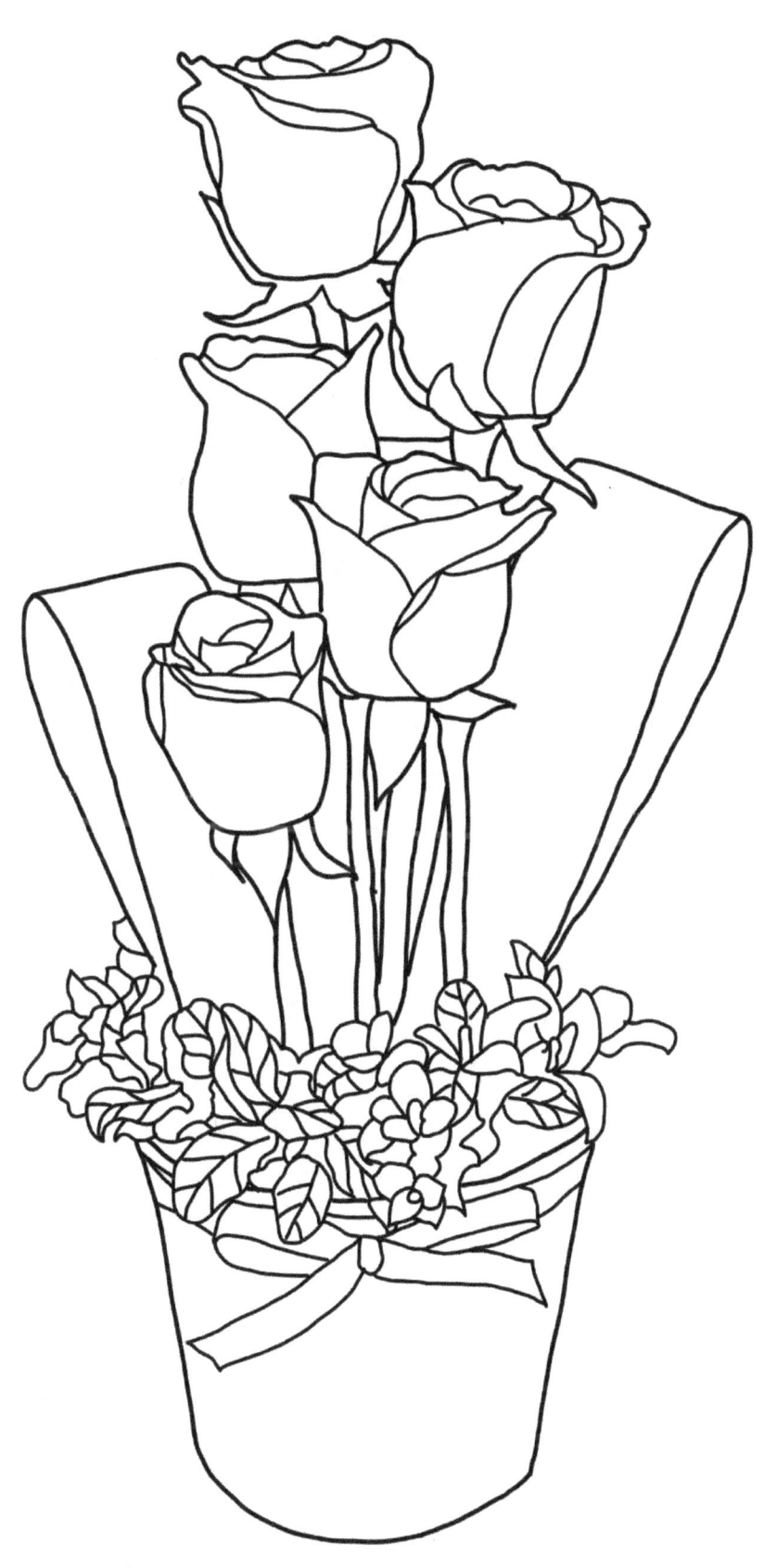

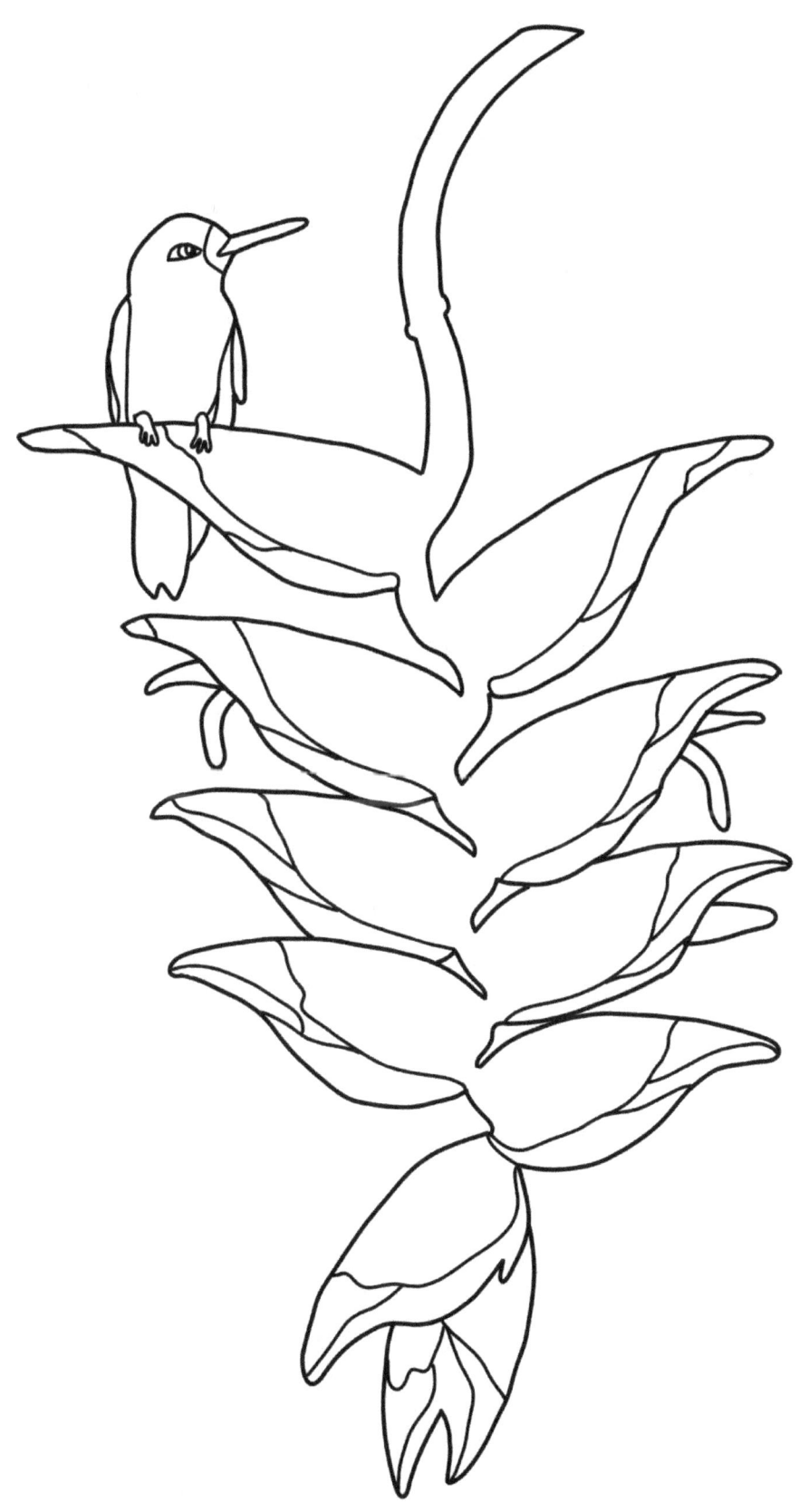

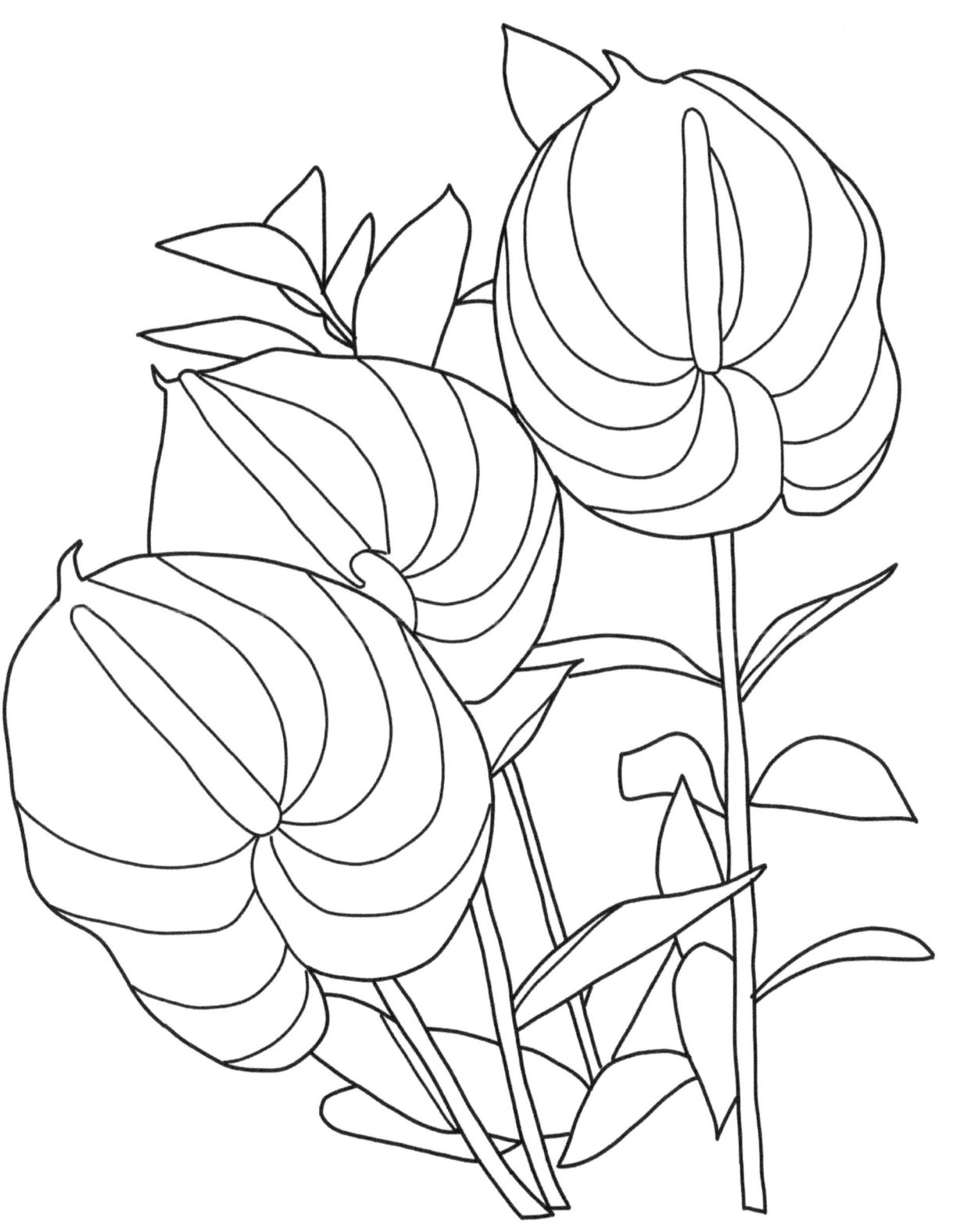

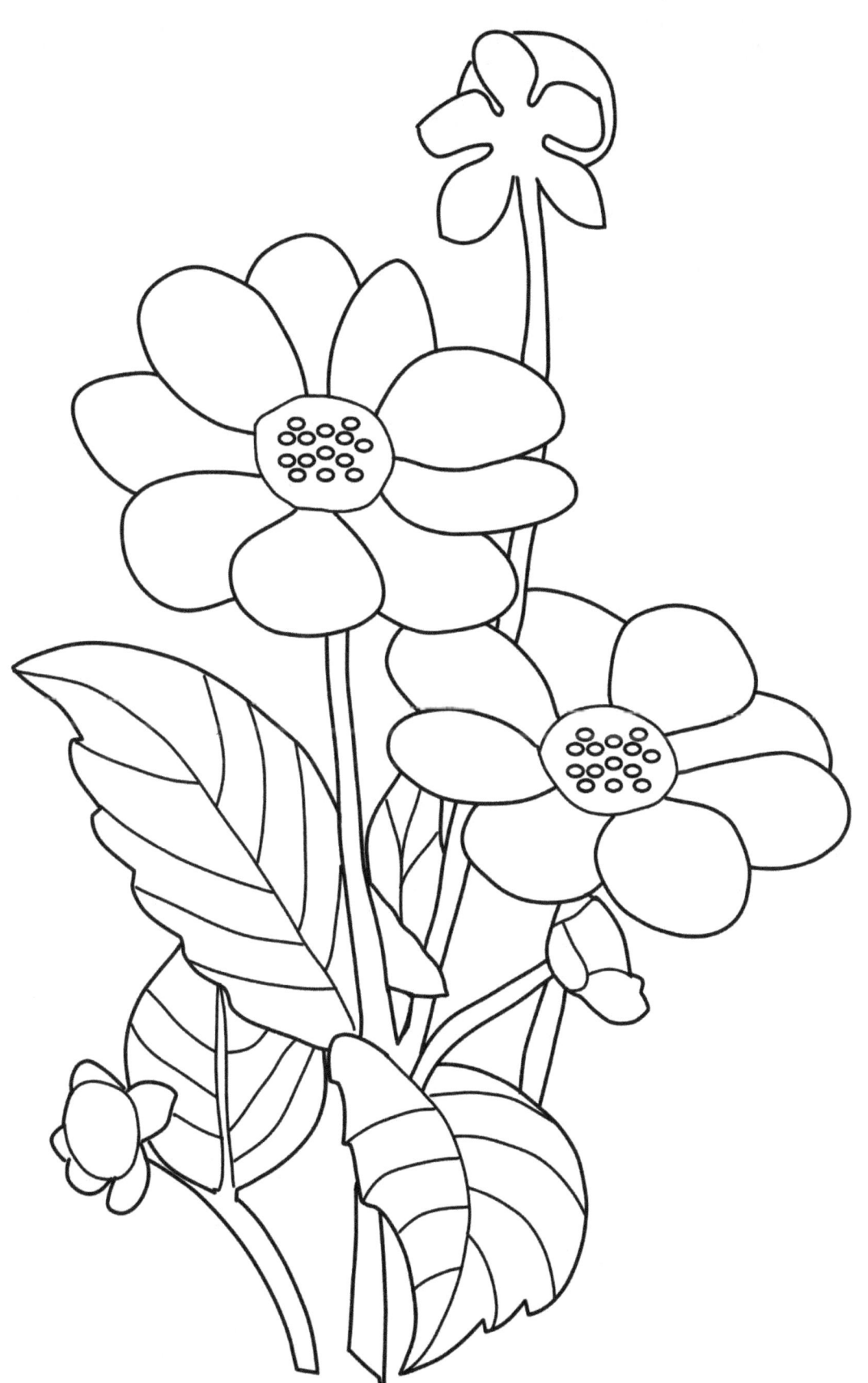

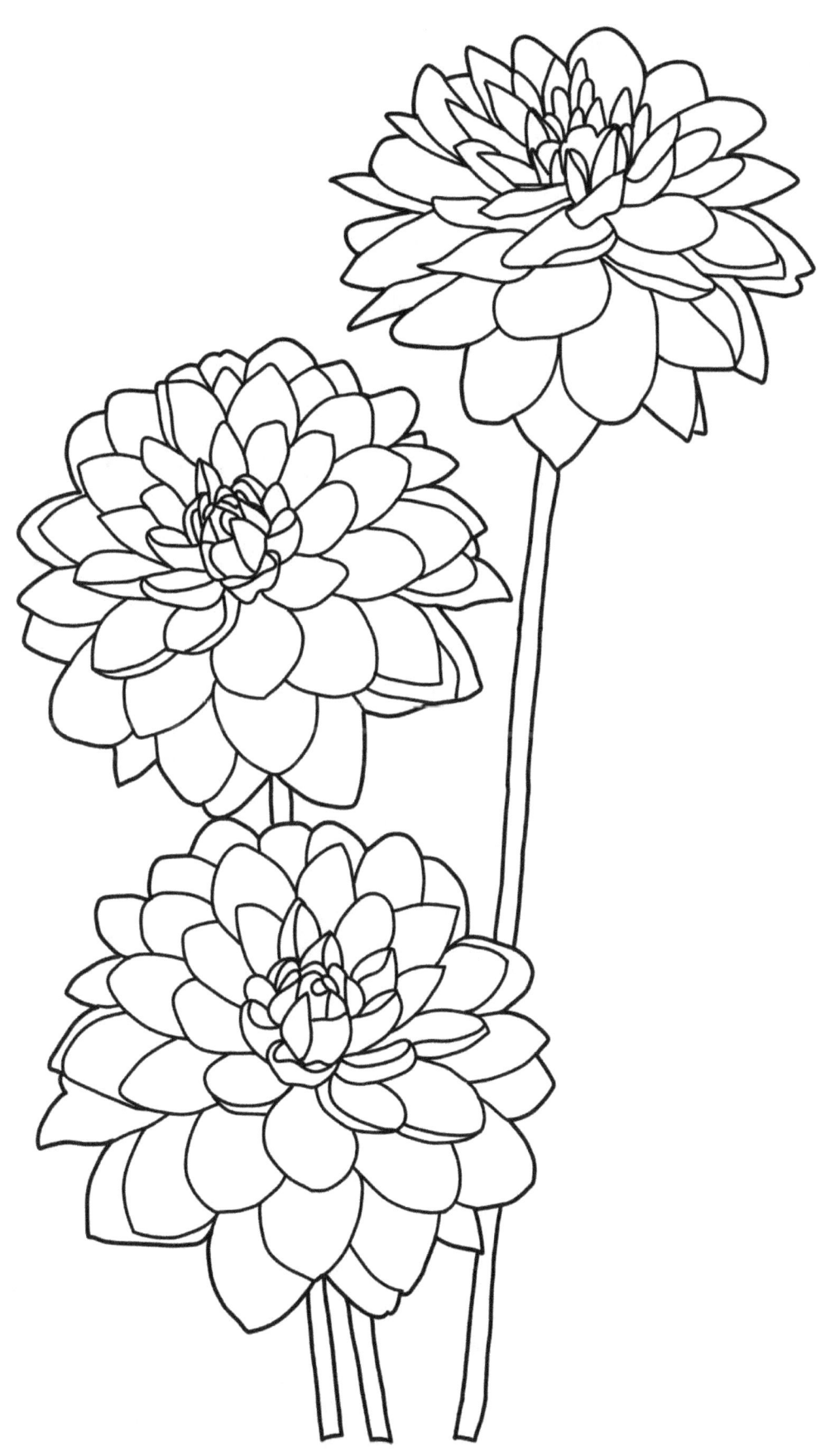

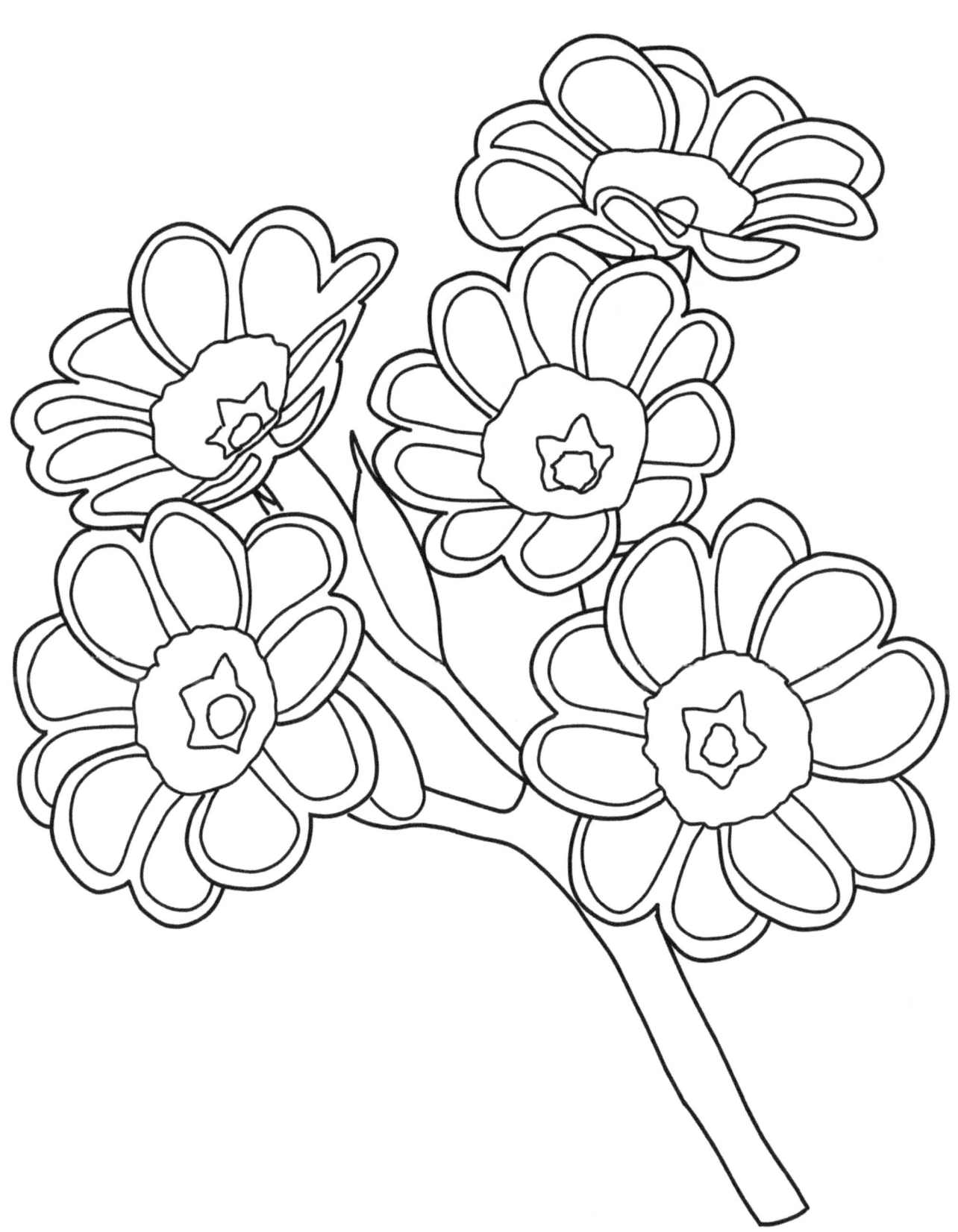

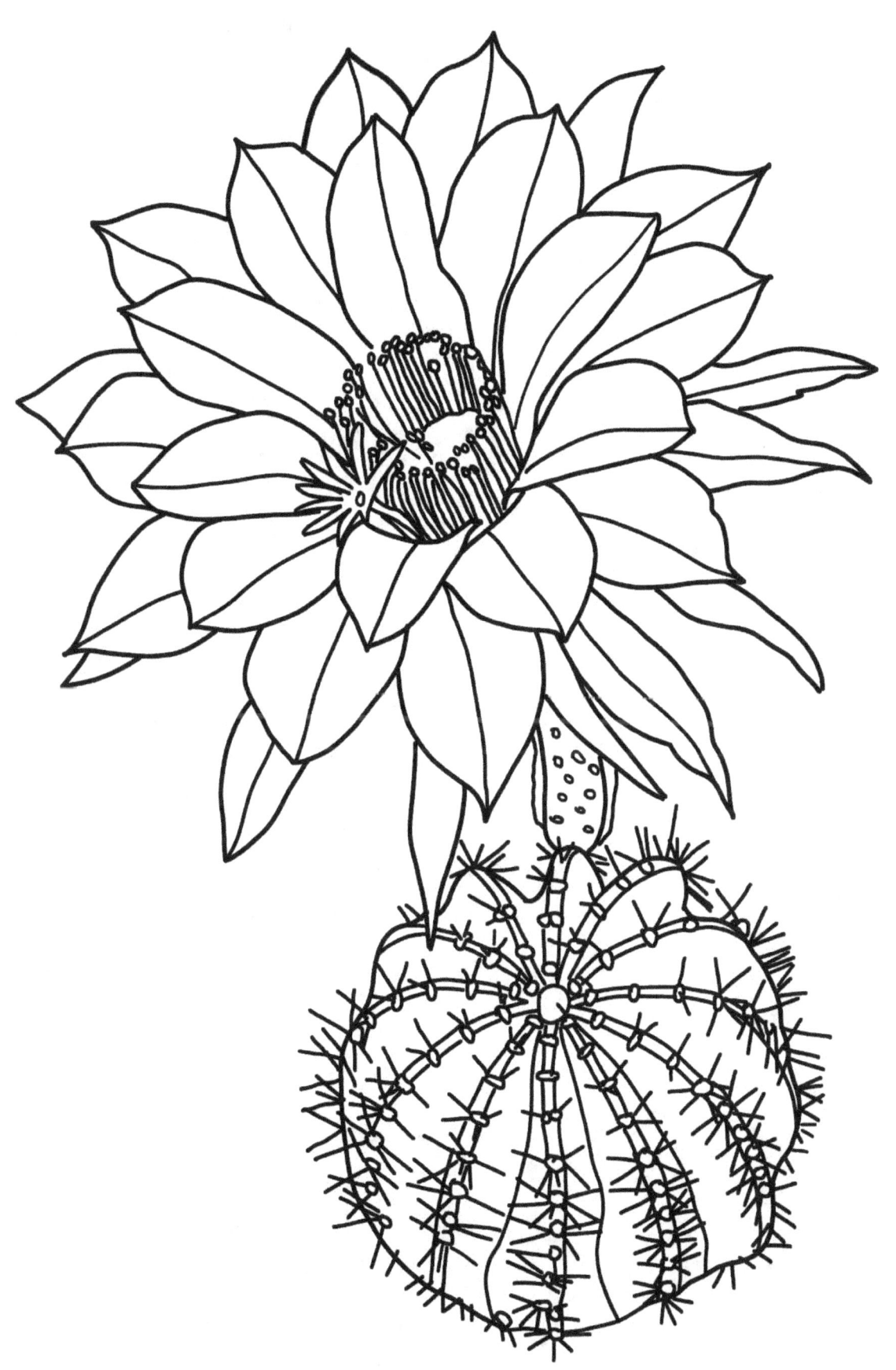

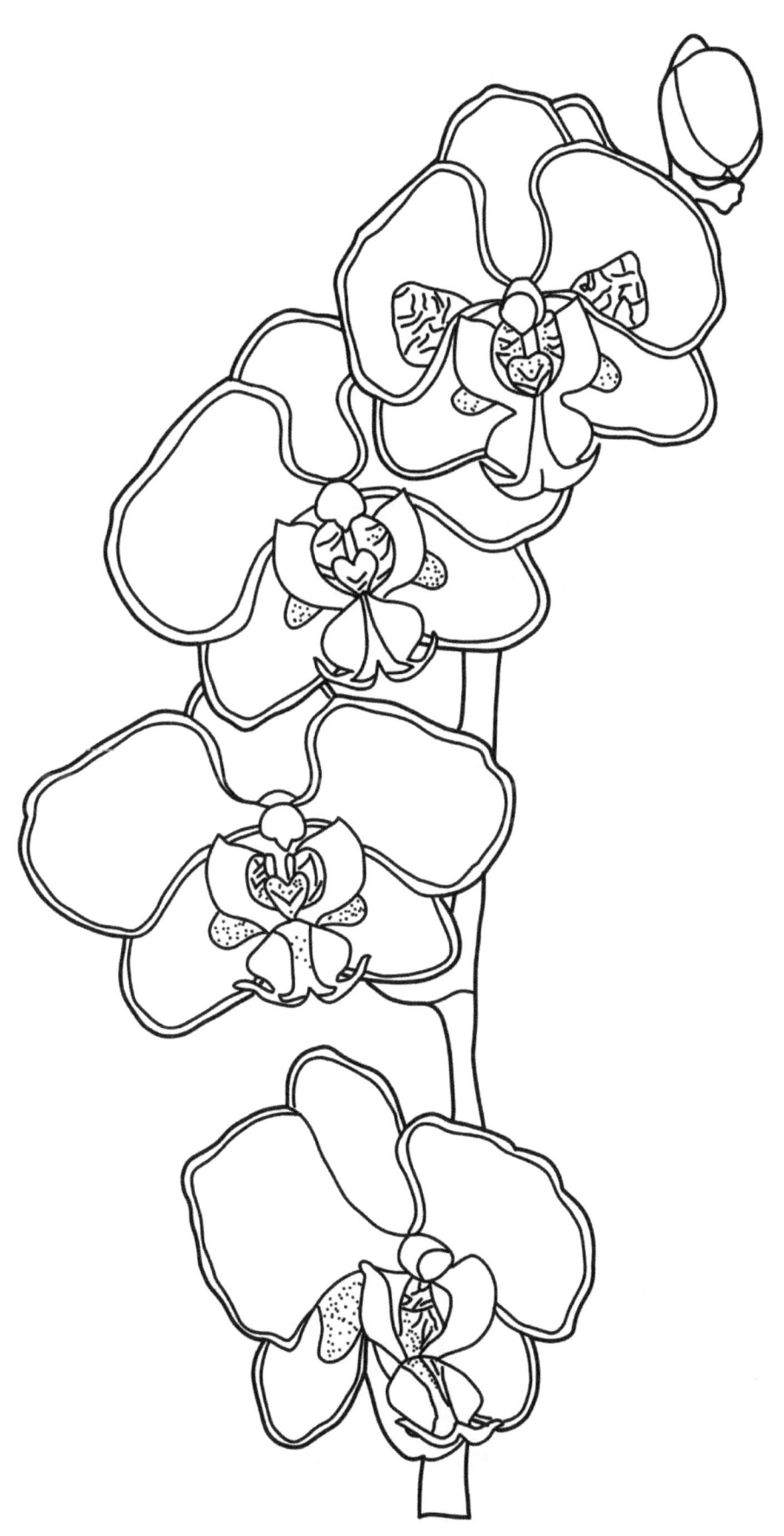

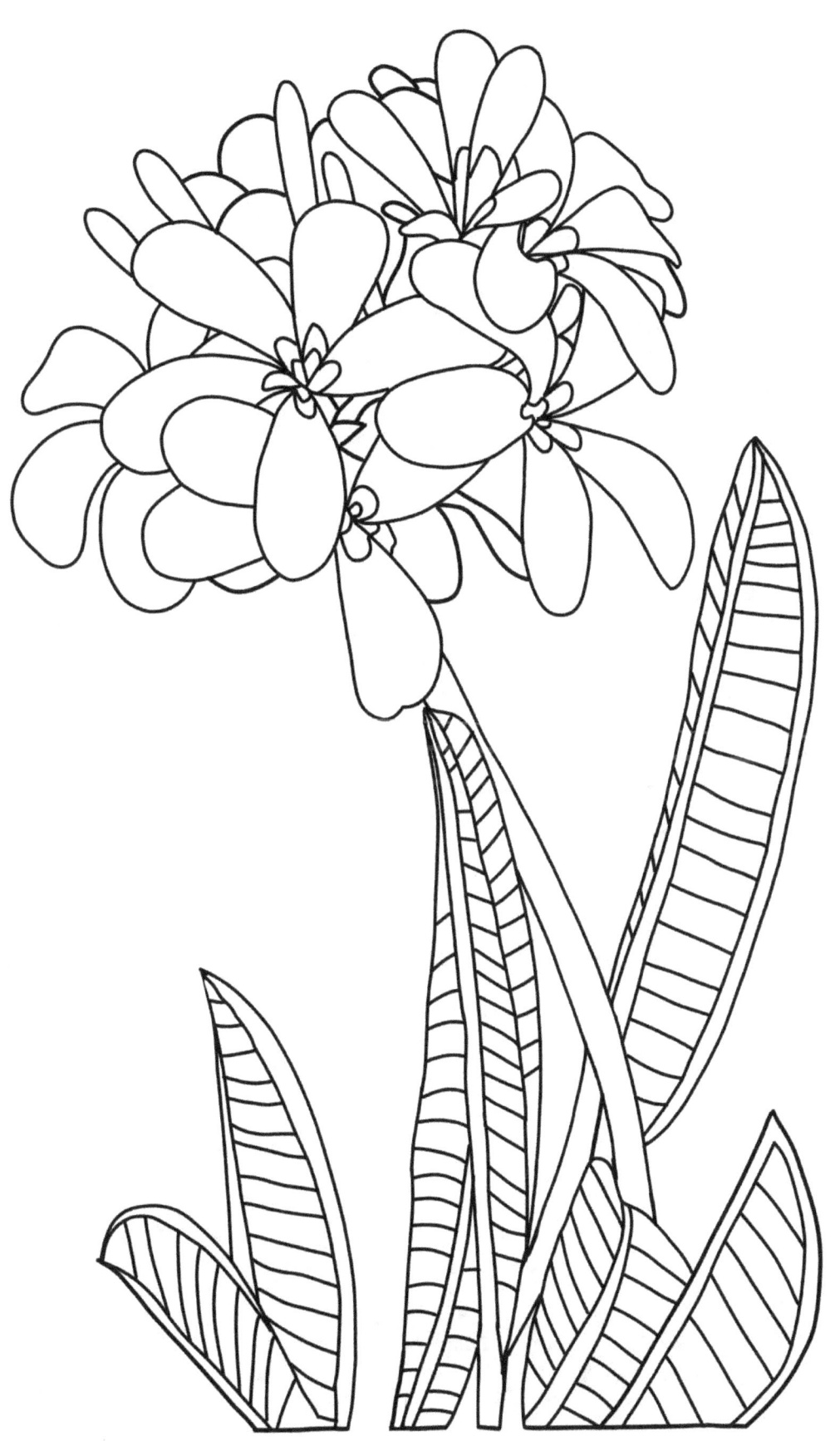

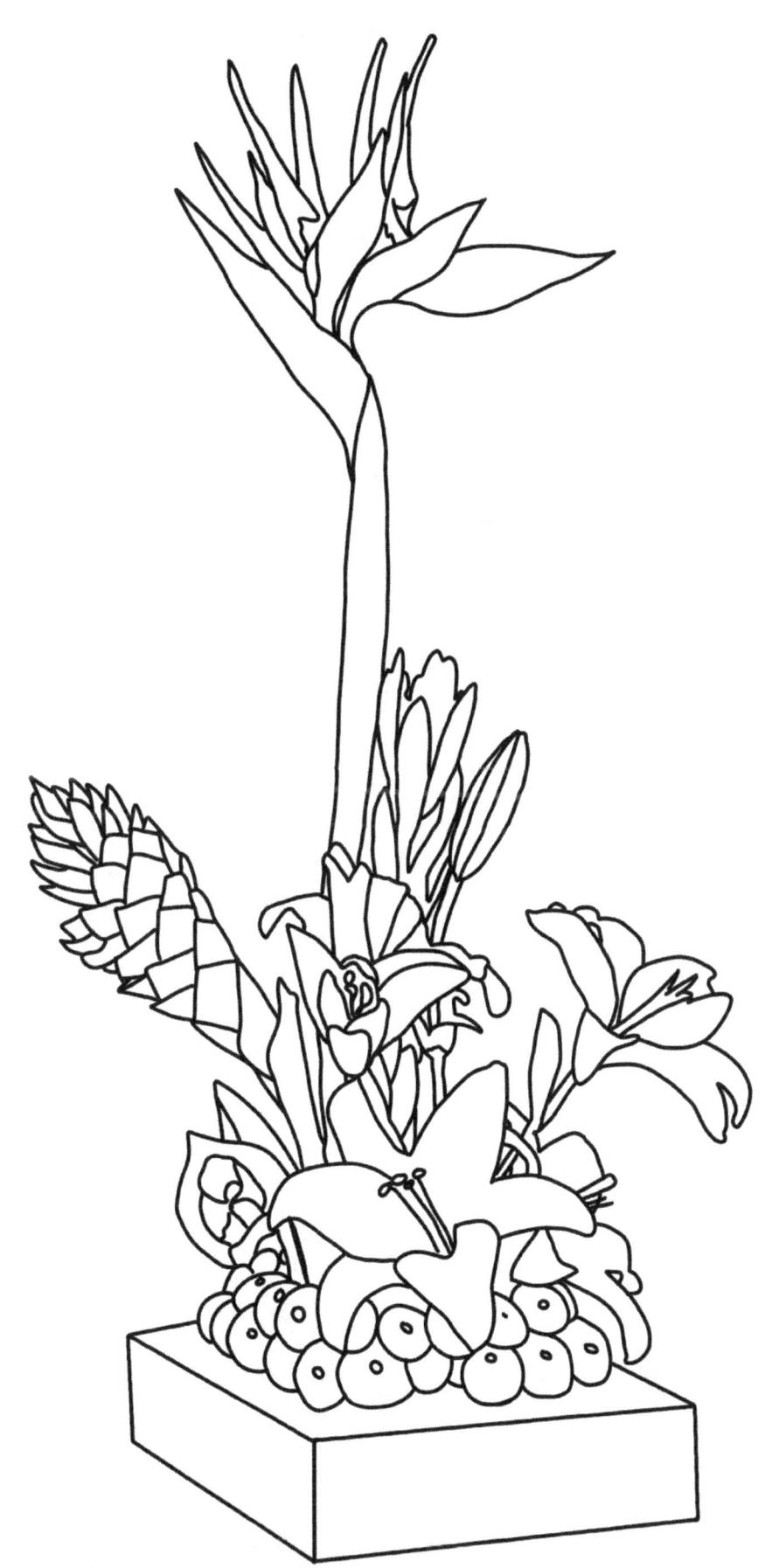

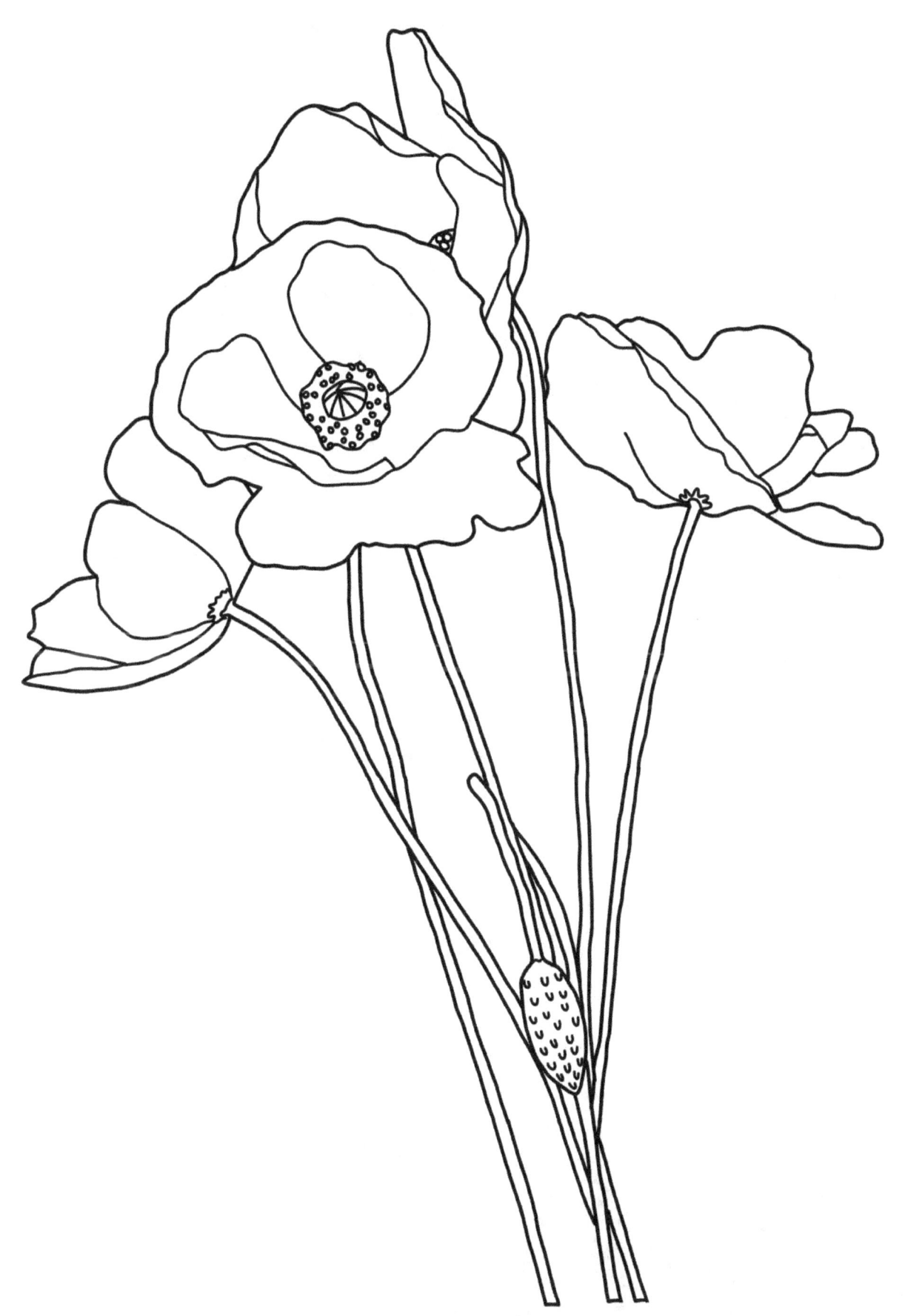

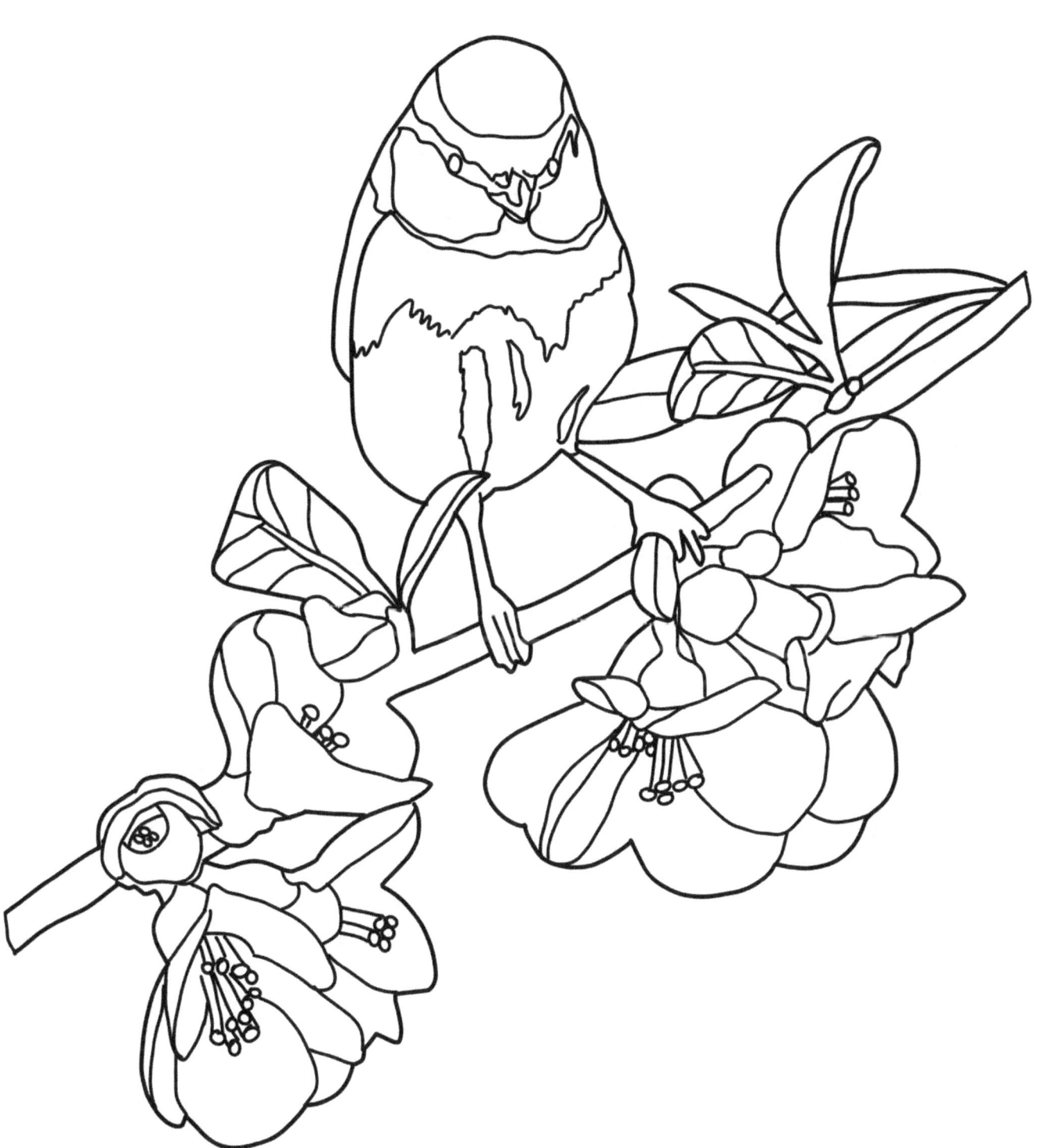

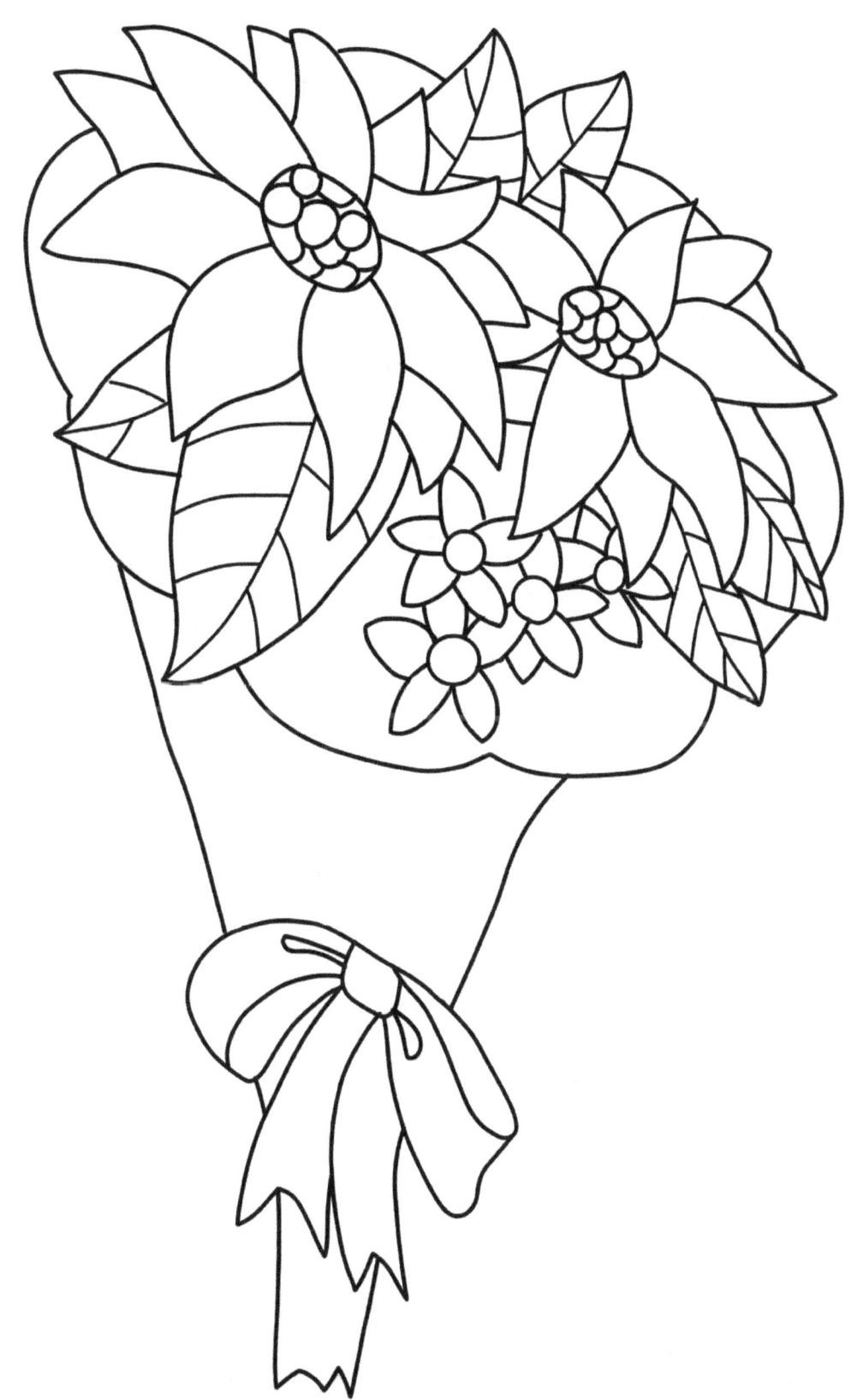

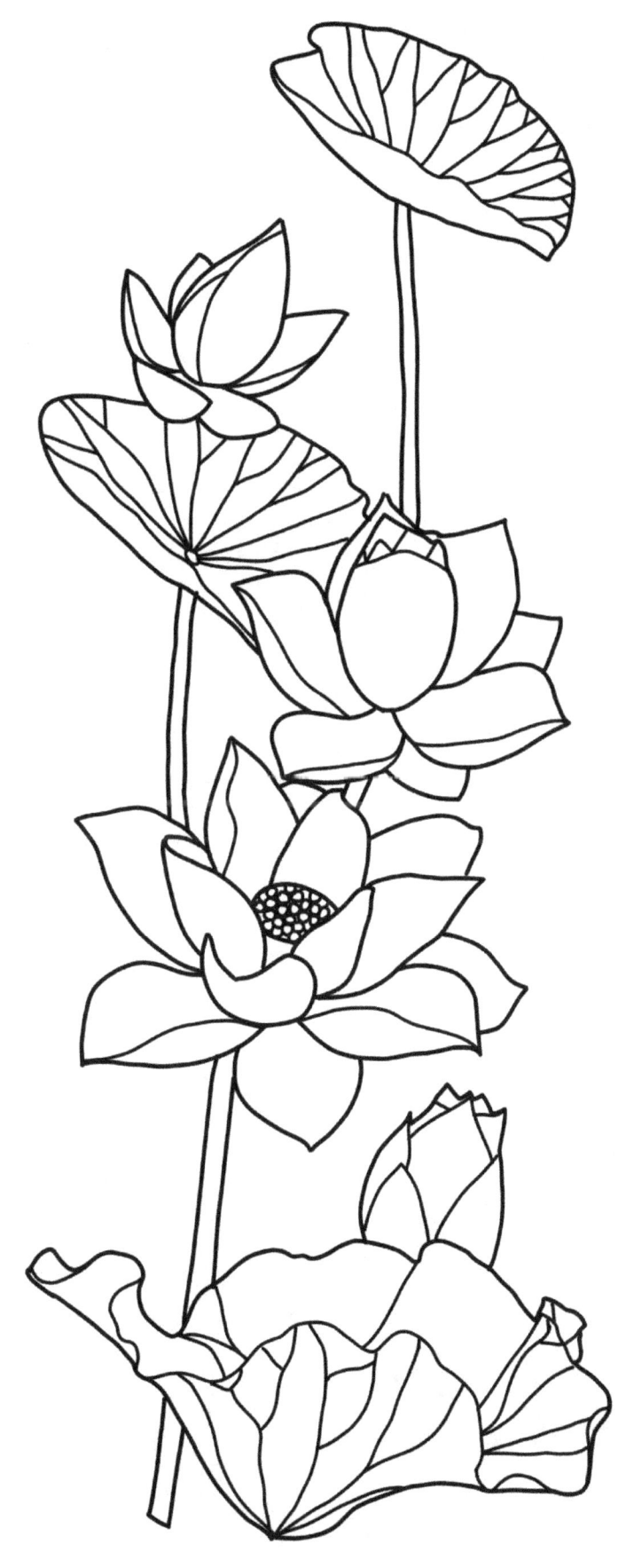

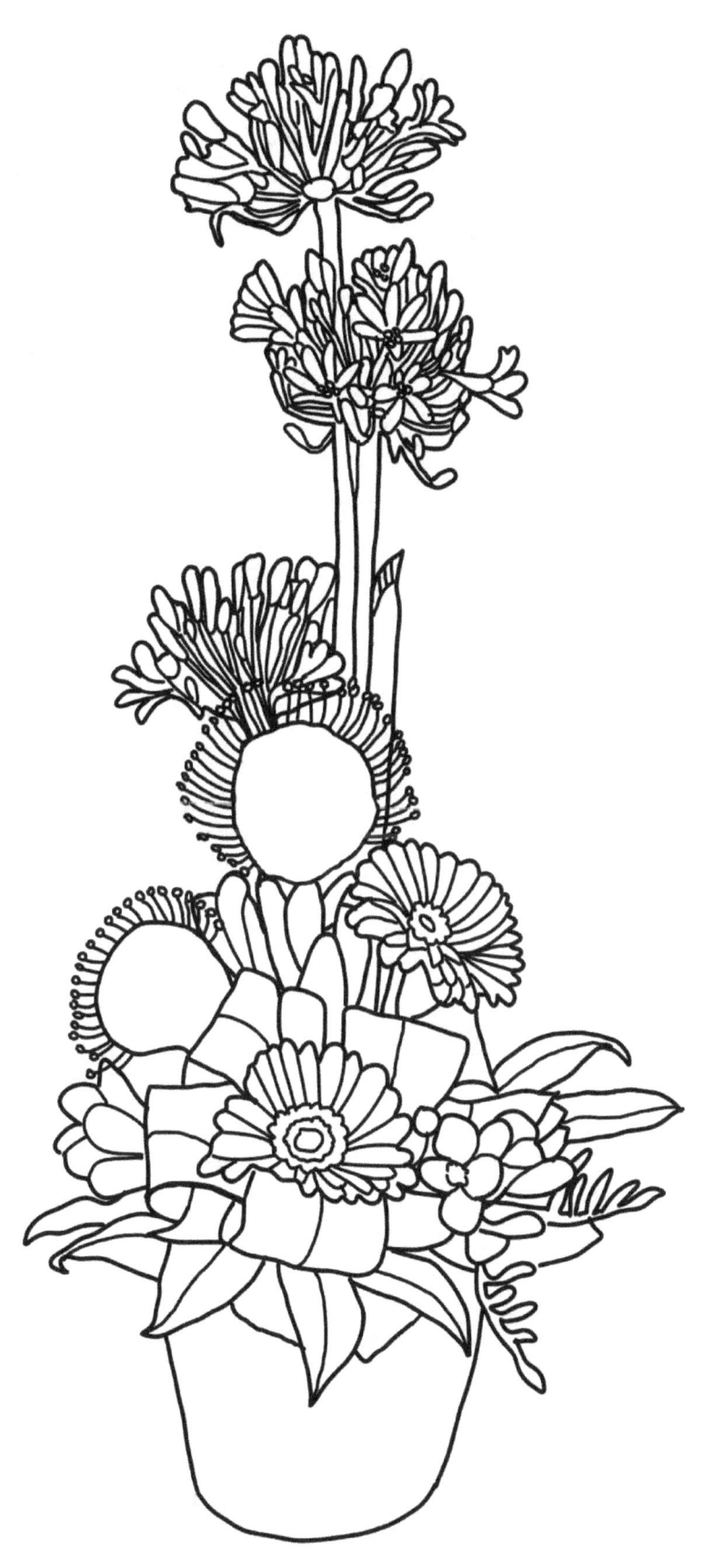

Flowers for You

Adult Coloring Book

This coloring book for adults is a compilation of beautiful hand drawn flowers dedicated to beginners, seniors and individuals with low vision. It includes thirty delightful floral illustrations designed in bolder print and one sided to avoid bleed-through and allow a relaxing and enjoyable coloring experience.

What a Colourful World

About Lupita Romo

Lupita Romo grew up in a family of artists. Both her parents inspired her to appreciate art and to follow her passion which eventually led her to complete a Bachelor Degree in Graphic Design and a University Diploma in Art. She likes bright colours and simple forms and loves art seen through the eyes of children. She enjoys sharing her passion by teaching art and the theory of colors to children and seniors alike.

Flowers for You
Adult Coloring Book

ISBN-13: **978-1546706977**
ISBN-10: **1546706976**

You may also like:

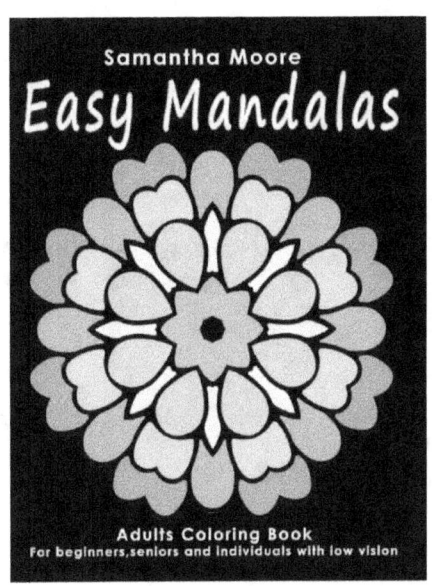

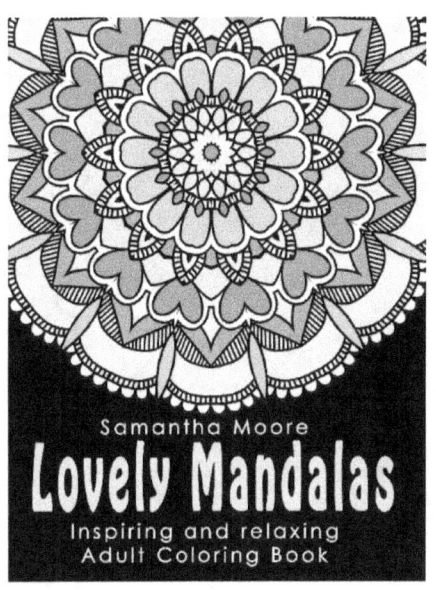

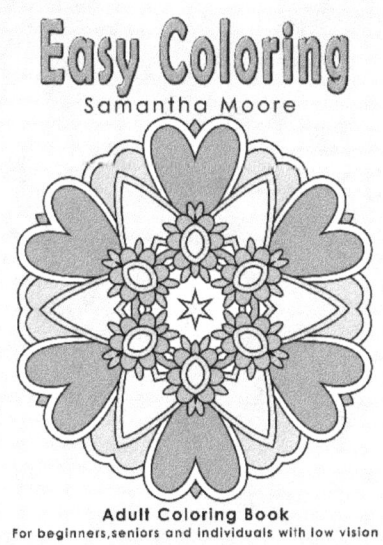

We would love to receive your comments. Please, find a moment to write a review on Amazon.

Thank you.